PAMELA HOLM is a writer and artist living in San Francisco. Her essays have been published in newspapers and magazines including the *San Francisco Chronicle*, *San Francisco Magazine*, and *The Denver Post*.

The Toaster Broke, So We're
# Getting Married

# The Toaster Broke, So We're
# Getting Married

A MEMOIR

PAMELA HOLM

VILLARD BOOKS Ⓥ NEW YORK

Library of Congress Cataloging-in-Publication Data

Holm, Pamela.
The toaster broke, so we're getting married : a memoir / Pamela Holm.
p.   cm.
Originally published: San Francisco : MacAdam/Cage Pub., 2002.
ISBN 0-8129-7025-X (alk. paper)
1. Holm, Pamela.   2. Married women—Biography.   3. Weddings—
Case studies.   I. Title.

HQ734.H77 A3 2002
306.872'3'092—dc22                                        2003068897

Villard Books website address: www.villard.com

Printed in the United States of America

9  8  7  6  5  4  3  2  1

Book design by Dorothy Carico Smith

*To Denzil*

# BEFORE

When Denzil and I moved in together I was just coming out of a writing hiatus that lasted longer than I'd planned. Now that the drama of single life had subsided my goals were very clear: I wanted to raise my daughter, write books and have a good relationship.

I carved writing time out of my days and guarded it greedily. Just as I was sinking into a rewrite of a shelved novel Denzil proposed to me and life immediately shifted into frantic wedding-planning mode.

I knew that the only way to stay sane during the process of getting married, and to not feel cheated out of my writing time, was to write about the wedding.

For six months I wrote about everything I thought and did. I wrote pages and pages, I filled notebooks, I scribbled on the backs of ATM receipts and napkins, anything I could get my hands on. At night I'd sit at my desk and knock out ranting e-mails to my friends about cake tasting or searching for wedding favors. Post-it notes with cryptic messages like "burn CD for dinner," and "a veil that makes me look like a beekeeper," and something illegible that looks like it says "trust is the bitter curse of poultry," were stuck to the walls around my desk like yellow fish scales.

Eventually these notes turned into essays, then the essays ganged up and turned into a book.

The Toaster Broke, So We're
# Getting Married

# I DO?

I had exactly twelve hours of post-engagement bliss. It lasted until Jessica, who had spent the past year planning her wedding, heard my announcement. She countered my news with the requisite shrill screams, rapidly followed by "Now you have to think about the date, and the place, and your dress, and the ring, and your hair, and the music, the food, cake, guests, invitations. Oh my God, you have so much to do!"

While I felt comfortable saying I'd spend the rest of my life with Denzil, I wasn't sure how we'd weather the relentless onslaught of joint decision-making that apparently lay ahead of us. I looked at my little jade engagement ring, then back at Jessica. I hadn't realized this was what getting married was about. I was still caught in the butterfly-wing fantasy of happily ever after, still surprised at the turn of events in my life. Still a little stunned that this was something I actually wanted to do. There was no gun to my head, no extenuating circumstances, nothing to cover for or legitimize. Denzil and I were getting married simply because we wanted to and simply because we were in love.

I had done this before, and there are no parts of my previous wedding I want to repeat. Not the waddling down the "aisle" six months pregnant with the pointy heels of my white pumps slipping through the slats of our redwood deck, not the part where my brother's chair breaks and he falls to the ground in the middle of the ceremony, not the gnawing fear that my parents would break into a drunken brawl at the reception; not the 110-degree weather and the feet like watermelons. None of it.

The day of my first wedding, sixteen years ago, my mother showed up six hours early to help. Helping meant sitting on the deck of our Appalachian-slum-style cabin in the Santa Cruz mountains, drinking gin and howling with laughter as her pregnant daughter decorated the dry grassy area around the deck with a dozen plastic pink flamingos and streams of pink crepe paper. When my future mother-in-law arrived I was in the kitchen, bulging out of a pair of shorts and a flannel shirt, and ironing my wedding dress, for which I'd spent an extravagant $75.

Gary and I had been together since I was eighteen and he was twenty-seven. We were happy in our punk rock, artist, crash-pad sort of way. It was the early '80s and bad attitudes and black clothes were fashionable. I was skinny and sallow and angry, and liked it that way. I listened to the Clash every morning while getting ready for my miserable job at the sign shop, where I'd spend the day using power tools and getting leered at by men who were either working on or working off some sort of substance abuse problem.

Though neither Gary nor I were interested in drugs

enough to actually do them, our world was populated by people who shifted between heroin addiction and speed binges. People who ran their cars into highway embankments, people who had to be bailed out of jail for breaking their neighbor's arm at a 4th of July barbecue, friends who threw up in the back seat of our car after raiding our medicine cabinet and taking everything they could find with sleepy eyes on the bottle. At the time, twenty-two and pregnant seemed as good a reason as any to get married.

The wedding was scheduled for 2:30. At around 2 o'clock my mom and I were crowded into the tiny bathroom. I was turned toward the clawfoot bathtub that had been jammed into one end of the shower stall. I could smell the gin on her breath as she wound strands of my shaggy hair around the barrel of a curling iron.

"I'm very proud of you," she said. I knew my mother was attempting to step up to the plate.

"You've done well for yourself. You have a good life here." A tiny green frog hopped out of the drain. I'd stopped flinching at the sight of frogs in my bathroom months ago.

"You're marrying a good man," she said. I wanted to grab the frog and kiss it. I wanted to believe this was the right choice. I wanted to believe I was embarking on a lifetime of happiness, but I knew there was as much chance of my being happy in this marriage as there was of that frog turning into a prince. My mom's hand slipped and the curling iron dropped onto my forehead, leaving a coffee-colored stripe seared into my skin. In lieu of any insightful commentary or advice, she combed my hair into a lopsided Lady Di do.

Our friends, most of whom looked like vampires, started to arrive dressed in their funereal best, draped in black suits and red velvet dresses, pale makeup and dark lips. They gathered on the slant of a dead grass hill under an oak tree, cowering from the sun while sipping champagne and fanning themselves with cocktail napkins. The minister, looking like he might drop dead from liver disease, heat prostration, or old age, leaned against his cane under the shade of the tree.

At 2:25 Gary rolled up and parked his '67 Volvo next to the oak tree. He had been delayed at the salon where his hair was being sculpted into a style normally reserved for small poodles. We took one look at each other and burst out laughing.

Inexplicably, my father chose this day to forget where I lived. Five minutes into the ceremony his Cadillac barreled up the dirt road in a cloud of dust. He and Susie, my stepmother, leapt out of the car panicked and disheveled. Until now I had understood the term "shotgun wedding" to mean something other than wanting to take a shotgun to your entire family.

The ceremony was a short, sweet blur that underscored the short, sweet blur of the bad idea that was our original decision.

After Cara was born my life changed beyond recognition. I wasn't working all day and staying up all night dancing with my friends. I was a mom. My days were filled with laundry and soap operas and a husband who worked ten-hour days and fell asleep on the couch every night. Our friends were getting in more and more trouble and the stakes were getting higher.

Living in the mountains with a baby proved to be isolating, so I joined a mothers' group, but when I realized the other mothers were even more confused and depressed than I was, I scrapped the group and started art school.

Things started to fall apart a few years into the marriage when the sweetness of motherhood and the fun of art school began to win out over waiting for my husband to come home from work and bailing our friends out of jail.

Gary's willingness to see the best in our messed-up friends held fast as mine diminished. When I left it was as much to get away from them as from a husband. But instead of rolling gracefully into a new and better life as I'd imagined, I was sideswiped by such incredible sadness that Gary was remarried with another child before I found my footing.

I spent the next twelve years actively avoiding marriage. My avoidance was fueled more by the desire not to get divorced than the desire to remain single. I couldn't bear the thought of dividing the record collection and divvying up the Tupperware again. I couldn't stand to forfeit another saucepan, and try to remember which books were mine and which I'd given to him as gifts. And I didn't want to have to explain to Cara that our world had just exploded, again.

Rather than take the more reasonable route of avoiding divorce by dating only men who were likely prospects for long-term commitment and family life, I took the alternate route of only dating men with whom there wasn't a chance in hell of a serious relationship.

Over the years my boyfriends tended to fall into two camps: those who wanted to save me from the desperate wilderness of single motherhood, and those who saw me as mommy and wanted to jump into the picture as child number two.

The list was long and diverse, with each guy being assigned some sort of semi-demeaning moniker to help my friends keep them straight when I called up whining.

There was the grocery store boy, the angry Irishman, the Welshman, the British Guy who quickly morphed into "That British Bastard." There was the twenty-four-year-old, the millionaire, the musician, the artist, the Venezuelan car dealer, the motorcycle guy, the tattoo guy, the not-very-bright guy, the codger, the D.J., and the guy with the dogs. Most of these relationships came and went rather quickly, with the exception of Cork, a.k.a. the artist.

Cork's effect on our lives was dramatic and irrevocable. He hijacked me and Cara out of San Jose, a place that had never felt like home, though until I met Cork I hadn't seen my way to leaving, as if the gates were locked.

He brought us to San Francisco and believed in me in a way no one ever had. I went from being an art student who made huge paintings and unwatchable performance art to traveling around the world installing Cork's work in museums and galleries. We stayed in the homes of people who owned the paintings and sculptures I'd been quizzed on in my art history classes for the past three years.

For six years we worked together and played together. Cork, Cara and I were the antithetical family, more a circus act than a cozy refuge from the outside world. Our house was a wall-to-wall museum of eclectica, and the rhythm of life was more a jazz solo than the soft cadence of a love ballad.

Even though laughter was the mainstay of our relationship, I was eventually worn down by Cork's nebulous but consuming depression, and the sad realization that without really meaning to I'd gone from artist to Cork's able assistant.

Aside from Cork, in the unlikely event that I began dating someone I actually liked, any ideas of a serious relationship were squashed by Cara, who was steadfastly bent on keeping me to herself. As long as a relationship was platonic she was a cherub, the smartest kid in the world, and the most beautiful, with a winning smile and quick wit. All these attributes quickly evaporated as soon as she saw a lingering look or an arm slipped around my waist. Actions which invariably prompted Cara to sprout horns and spit fire.

The few times I tried integrating someone else into our lives the results ranged from mildly troubling–Cara turning the offending boyfriend's toothbrush upside down into the scum at the bottom of the toothbrush cup –to disastrous–Cara pounding up and down the hallway at 1 a.m. shouting "I-want-him-out-of-my-house-now!" punctuating each word with a firm stomp.

After several years of disastrous dating scenarios–men who "forgot" to tell me about their wives or girlfriends, men who cried on first dates, men who told me they were in love then didn't call for three weeks–I began to suspect I emitted a silent signal, like a dog whistle, audible only to men with serious mental health issues. Psychotics and criminals, philanderers and commitment-phobes. Guys with long-standing depression, orphans in search of their birth mothers, men still in love with their exes, disbarred lawyers, crestfallen artists. A barrel full of monkeys.

Apart from my own dismal experiences of dating and holy matrimony, I had the memories of my parents' various divorces and breakups to help keep at bay any fleeting desire to get married again. My parents were of the generation that married too soon to know whether or not they liked each other. It didn't take them long to figure out they didn't. It did, however, take fourteen years of mutual misery before they decided to throw in the towel. They split up in 1971 when divorce suddenly became acceptable, even fashionable. I was ten and my brothers were six and twelve. The shift in our lives was foreshadowed by my father's lamb-chop sideburns and my mother's sudden penchant for purple corduroy hip-huggers and fuzzy velour jumpsuits.

My mother was well-suited to single life. She continued with her steady routine of laundry, cooking and bed-making, and seemed to effortlessly incorporate a forty-hour work-week at a camera store. She was suddenly empowered with the first dizzying effects of women's lib. Billie Jean King and Helen Reddy, burn your bra and throw the bum out. She carried out the fine-print instructions on the contract of her new life with grace, humming "I Am Woman", while making the transition from housewife to single working mother.

While my mom adjusted to her new life with the support of an entire nation, my father didn't fare so well. The fine print on his side of the divorce said no furniture, no hot meals, and the release of a tether that sent him sailing out of orbit on all-night benders, bar fights and a rapid-fire turnover of girlfriends, each nuttier than her predecessor.

Less than a year after the divorce my father married Linda, a buxom redhead with four kids. When we were all in the same house there were seven of us between the ages of seven and thirteen. We were the anti-Brady Bunch. We lit things on fire and shoplifted. We played darts in the living room and slid down the stairs on an upturned coffee table. We had raucous fights over which television show to watch. It was heaven. The fact that the marriage lasted two years was somewhat of a miracle.

For the next five or six years my brothers and I were bounced back and forth between our parents and their current lovers or spouses. There was Angie, the twenty-eight-year-old sex kitten/cocktail waitress with a killer wardrobe and two overweight children. Life with Angie was always volatile. She could turn from charming best friend into shrewish competitor with the bat of an eye. She and my father tormented each other at close range on and off for a couple of years. My brothers spent those years wondering what she looked like with her clothes off. I spent them praying she would move out, but leave her clothes with me.

When my dad and Angie finally broke up things just got worse. He hooked up with a woman named Elaine who worked as the bookkeeper for his plumbing business. When the relationship hit a rocky patch Elaine registered her displeasure by tossing the account books out the window of her Pinto on the highway before calling the IRS to have him audited.

The lineup on my mother's side wasn't much better. First there was Marty, who took me for Sunday drives when I was twelve. He half-impressed and half-terrified me going 90 m.p.h. on the highway while inching his hand up my thigh. Then there was Saul, the Jewish stockbroker with a cardigan for every occasion: driving, mowing the lawn, eating dinner. For years my mother was involved with her boss Jay, who once climbed through my bedroom window in the middle of the night, then sat at the end of my bed, drunk and in tears, complaining that my mom wouldn't answer his phone calls.

The fear of leaving another glaring pockmark on my marital record, combined with Cara's behavior, the caliber of men I ran up against, and a scrapbook full of bad memories, made it easy to stay single, or at least my own mutated, high-traffic version of single.

# THE LAST FIRST DATE

Denzil and I tell conflicting stories of our first meeting. He swears I was dressed in white; I know I was wearing black crushed velvet. Denzil claims we met in November. I'm certain we met at a Christmas party, a huge warehouse affair that was a fundraiser for Burning Man, a week-long festival of absurdity in the Nevada Desert. Music blared and girls in white knee-boots and Santa hats flitted around like oversexed elves.

Denzil and I caught each other's eye but by now I'd learned to exhibit a polite disinterest in strangers, to say hello but keep moving. I had also learned to be wary in this group. Because you tended to only see these people at parties, you were never quite sure how they would translate into real life.

This was a welcoming scene, almost too welcoming. Newcomers were treated like alien abductees. The moment your fresh face showed up at a party you were circled and questioned and flirted with. You were probed and prodded as they tried to ascertain your status; single, married, corruptible?

The people in this crowd are like stops on a train: sooner or later you're bound to pass through all of them. Flash, the wildman who'll bless and curse you in the same hoarse Rhode Island growl. Kim, the pink-haired Space Cowgirl with a crass mouth and a line of clothing made from fake fur and Astroturf. Jerry James, who'll tell you he built the first Burning Man. Jeffrey, a lanky Texan who'll spin yarns about elegant candlelit parties he's staged in abandoned bunkers, or a three-state police chase that ended with him stealing a police car then running for three days and nights through the Texas prairie in handcuffs. There's Louise, the seamstress who costumes herself in themes rather than simply getting dressed, then belies this frivolity by insisting on talking about Noam Chomsky or the book she just read on physics or Chinese economics. Miss P, the matriarch of the community, who holds court with the languishing demeanor of the caterpillar in *Alice in Wonderland*.

You had to be careful who you became friendly with in this crowd or you might end up watching fireworks from a structural tower of the Bay Bridge and then spending the night in jail. Or find yourself rampaging the city with fifty drunken Santas loaded into a silver school bus, followed by a night in jail. Or marching in the Saint Stupid's Day parade dressed as members of a suicide cult. Or spending Bastille Day dressed as Marie Antoinette and feeding cake to homeless people in Golden Gate Park. It was common knowledge to anyone who'd been around for a while that these were the people to party with, not date.

I was facing the stage watching a transvestite in gold lamé and a wheelchair sing "Santa Baby," when Denzil showed up beside me.

"What do you think?" he asked, tipping his chin toward the stage.

I nodded, "He's good."

"She," Denzil corrected, "I think he's a she."

"Right. I'm never sure how that works."

"Denzil," he said, extending his hand. "How do you know these people?"

"I'm not sure anymore. How about you?"

"Most of them are my friends."

Denzil was thin and fit and beautiful. His features were angular and defined. His olive skin was smooth and perfect. I leaned to one side to get a better look at his dark eyes, made smaller by the lenses of his wire-rimmed glasses.

I'm of average height, with pale skin and blue eyes that sometimes seem to frighten people. My hair has been hennaed red so long I can't remember what color it's supposed to be. But if it weren't for my nose, which looks as if it's been broken, and my wardrobe that never really graduated from art school, I could probably pass myself off as an ordinary soccer mom.

"What do you do when you're not watching transvestites sing Christmas songs?" I asked. As Denzil spoke I stared absentmindedly at his lips and found it impossible to concentrate on what he was saying. My attention drew in and out. Beautiful teeth–*focus groups in Cleveland, Ohio*–beautiful eyes–*eleven-year-old Pokemon collectors*–tall and lean–*television's role in society*–damn he's good-looking. Charming, articulate, confident and employed, a novelty for this group.

In ten minutes Denzil had shattered the stereotypes I'd spent the past several years building. I'd come to expect good-looking and vapid to go hand in hand and it didn't always bother me that much. I find beauty intoxicating and probably much more important than I ought to. I'd dated plenty of men for the sheer enjoyment of looking at them, but the thrill was starting to wear off.

"You wanna have coffee sometime?" Denzil asked.

By now everything around me had dropped into soft focus and I could almost forget about my boyfriend Matt on the other side of the room, and the other guy I was seeing who wasn't really my boyfriend but with whom I had an "arrangement."

"Sure," I answered dreamily.

Matt and I had an open relationship, which meant we were free to torture each other without guilt. It wasn't my idea. From the start Matt made it clear that he wasn't interested in a monogamous relationship, describing his feelings with the pathetic metaphor "I love strawberry ice cream, but I don't want to eat it every day." Because I liked him, and because I wasn't having much luck going about relationships by any conventional means, I was willing to believe there might be a different way to succeed in romance.

In theory this arrangement sounded like one big love-fest. Spread the love around, the more the merrier, a world without jealousy or hate. In theory we were going to overcome pettiness and competition. In theory we were going to have all the different flavors of ice cream we wanted.

All this was great until I found out that the theory had a face and a name, Marianne, a name that produced a severe laxative effect in me anytime I heard it. All of my open-minded hippie-wannabe calculations fell flat. I was tormented with jealousy and rage, made worse by the fact that I'd just denounced jealousy and rage.

Denzil gave me his phone number. I tucked it into

my pocket and tried to forget about his smile, which had quickly catapulted itself to the top of my list of favorite sights. I never called. I knew better than to pull him into our messy playground.

A few months later I ran into Denzil at a Valentine's Day party.

"Do you still have my number?" he asked.

"Yes," I said, but still didn't call.

By now Matt and I had backpedaled into a traditional monogamous relationship that so far wasn't working any better than our tumultuous stint at non-monogamy.

Several months down the road, after Matt had become an ex and the embarrassment of the whole thing subsided, Denzil invited me and Cara to a dinner party with some mutual friends.

I was happily surprised when the dinner invitation came our way. By now I'd had several opportunities to speak with Denzil and each time I'd come away feeling silly that I hadn't brought my life to a screeching halt and gone out with him when he asked me the first time.

"Try to be polite," I whispered to Cara, who was now fourteen and slightly less acidic than she was at twelve and thirteen, as we climbed the three flights of stairs up to Denzil's beautiful Victorian flat.

"I'll try," Cara responded as we made our way down the long hallway oohing and ahhing at the elegant details, the stained-glass windows, hand-carved banisters and the dark wood wainscoting that lined the hallway.

"It's nicer than our house," Cara pointed out.

"That's not hard, sweetie."

At the time we were living in a hollowed-out log. Our flat was dark and cold with a long windowless hallway. My office was in the coat closet under a stairwell. Our roommate, Janie, was an Oxford-grad genius who could help Cara with her math homework but couldn't operate the washing machine. She thought nothing of borrowing my underwear or breaking a window when she'd lost her keys.

Cara and I found our way to the kitchen where Denzil was standing at the sink, cleaning shrimp. I walked straight for him, wrapped my arms around his waist and asked, "Will you marry me?" A single man of thirty-seven rattling around in a large, nearly empty house sent a certain message. I once dated a man who owned one fork and one cup and slept in a single bed. He had a message, too.

By the time Denzil served dessert, Cara was figuring out the bus route from his house to her school. I took this as a good sign. More than a good sign. I was ready to faint into Denzil's arms based on this alone. I thought it wise to trust Cara's opinion, figuring that her male character radar, unlike my own, hadn't been tarnished by years of misuse. Before we left, Denzil and I made a date for the next weekend.

Relationships by this point had become a near constant sore spot for me. I seemed to be always getting in or getting out of the next big thing. Usually around the time I decided a relationship was good, the guy I was seeing decided it was over. Likewise, if I decided I wasn't interested in the person I was dating, this was generally his cue to connect himself to me like a barnacle. These light bulb "Oh my God I can't stand this guy" realizations were guaranteed to come at the most inconvenient times. Like halfway into a long weekend with 300 miles and another day and a half between the dismal discovery and being able to do anything about it. As familiar as this pattern became, I was still able to greet each new upset with fresh surprise.

I never learned to avoid prickly situations entirely, but I eventually got to where I could spot trouble coming, and learned to act accordingly.

Accordingly could mean running headlong into a doomed relationship with the enthusiasm of an idiot puppy. Or vanishing at the first flicker of anything I perceived to be hedging, anything to clear the floor before the object of my affection walked into the room with the deadened glimmer of someone who has just lost interest. With Denzil I was determined not to come on too strong and to keep my overzealous protection reflex at bay.

After a few months of dating I stopped trying to gauge how much to open my heart to Denzil and for how long. A few months after that I stopped sleeping with clenched fists. I started to believe that Denzil's professions of love held weight and substance.

Over the next several months, Denzil and I endured all the built-in tests that the natural progression of a relationship provides: the weekend away, the family dinner, running into the exes, the eight-hour flight with an unexpected layover in some faraway airport. We moved smoothly through the contemporary mating rituals: the ceremonial drawer-clearing, the safe-sex talk, the tandem AIDS test. We cleared one hurdle after the other, leaping over obstacles with room to spare. No skinned knees, no tumbling wipeouts. Not only did we endure, we thrived.

# THE MERGER

After dating for around six months, Denzil and I started talking about living together. The talks stalled out when I told him that I had no interest in moving in with someone unless I was planning to marry him. I couldn't see any reason to shack up with a boyfriend if both of us didn't have intentions of sticking around forever or somewhere thereabout. Also, marriage, or the threat thereof, was a way to assess my own level of commitment. It would be easy to move in together and let the years tick past, but if frivolous fun was what I was after I'd stay in the holding pattern I'd been in for the past several years.

I didn't see the point of disrupting Cara, packing up our fully functioning life, getting rid of my salad spinner and dish rack, if I was only going to have to rebuild the whole damn thing a couple of months or years down the road. Besides, I had plans for the future. I was going to get Cara through high school, pack my car and drive someplace warm and cheap where I could paint and write and dance.

This conversation sent Denzil into a two-month silence on the topic of living together. When the shock wore off the talks resumed with a knowing edge that implied marriage, but still wasn't quite ready to confront it straight on. We talked about our life together, we talked about the possibility of having more children. We talked about joint savings accounts, and moving to the other side of the world together. We talked about how to keep a marriage from becoming boring or destructive, though it was something neither of us knew much about. (Denzil has also been married before. His marriage can best be described as catastrophic.) We talked about Cara leaving for college and what we would do with all that freedom. But we never talked about getting married. The following January Cara and I moved into Denzil's house.

During our first month of living together, Denzil and I walked around with halos of exploding hearts crowning our heads. We kissed every time we passed in the hall and lovingly took each other's phone messages.

The idea of traditional family life had never held much interest for me, but with Denzil I began to see possibilities I'd never seen before. I saw a version of family that I not only found palatable, but one that I wanted to be part of. We had dinner at a table where we all laughed and were nice to each other, in a house where we argued about the meanings of words late into the night. We cooked, and cleaned the garage, and played Scrabble. All the things I swore I hated, I found myself doing with sunshine in my stomach.

Then just as we were settling into the sweet business of our new life, Denzil and I began noticing things about each other. Little things. Little, really annoying things. Soon Denzil began to register his complaints, subtly at first, pointing out things he thought I should know, like:

"Did you mean to leave the clothes in the dryer?" Next he started making requests. Asking me to close the lid on the toilet, asking me and Cara to hang up our coats when we came into the house, and not to leave our bags on the chair in the entry, and to keep the sharp knives out of the dishwasher. Denzil's requests weren't unreasonable, but I was astonished at how difficult they were to perform. It had been a long time since anyone had asked me to amend my behavior, and my natural reaction was to become stubborn and resentful.

Around the six-week mark, the merger began to feel like a hostile takeover. There was no lack of love, but the fact that we were annoying the hell out of each other was getting in the way of our expressing it. It wasn't just about love anymore, it was about laundry and garbage and wet towels and who put the spoons in the dishwasher upside down. I was proving to be an incurable slob, and he an incurable nag. The hearts in our halos began to deflate.

Cara's transition was flawless. She painted her room bright green and had slumber parties every weekend like any fifteen-year-old. She talked on the phone and did her homework and tuned out the bickering that rang through our hall.

But while Denzil was spared Cara's mischief, Cara and I were not spared his. Family life seemed to be turning Denzil into an amalgam of Robert Young, Felix Unger, and both of our mothers. Evenings, he walked around the house chanting a litany of domestic soundbites: "Doesn't anyone turn off lights around here?" and "Is the floor where we keep wet towels now?"

It was easy to understand Denzil's frustration. Two women had just stormed his beach and set up camp. Every scrap of open space was now overtaken with the refuse of feminine life. Our extensive collection of half-used cosmetics now crowded his shaving cream, razor and toothbrush to the top shelf of the medicine cabinet, a shelf now also occupied by nail polish and makeup brushes. Drawers that once held Band-Aids and Q-tips were now a dangerous tangle of hair ties, barrettes, and jewelry. Lace tablecloths and doilies settled on flat surfaces like locusts. Kitschy figurines and gaudy vases were strewn across countertops, windowsills and mantelpieces. Denzil's tastefully obscure pieces of art were now overshadowed by loud paintings and yellowing junkstore flower prints. The flood of household additions gave his formerly minimalist decor the feel of a 1950s garage sale.

As Denzil discovered what it meant to share a house with two women, I was making my own discoveries. First, that I had fallen in love with a man who worries about the egg stains on his Calphalon frying pan, and second, that I had been left to my own devices for long enough to become uncivilized. For years it had just been Cara and me. No real adults around to please, or even take into consideration. Just us and years of freedom. We spent those years happily tossing our damp towels on the floor, eating dinner in front of "Seinfeld" and leaving the dishes for later.

In the old days I slept alone, but the warmth of human contact was made up for by the layers of stray clothing that blanketed my bed. Aside from the lonely days, and lonely nights and mornings, and an overall feeling of emptiness—aside from being miserable—I think I was really quite happy.

After the second month of cohabitation, Cara and I showed signs of progress: dishes in the dishwasher, coats on the hook, shoes in the closet. Yet we happily backslid when Denzil left town for a couple of days on a business trip. Before his plane had left the ground, damp towels were draped on doorknobs, discarded bras and sweaters were tossed on the backs of chairs. After two days the kitchen was dressed in a familiar mess. All this happened through a strange alchemical process called laziness.

At around the ten-week mark, after a high-volume exchange, and a series of conversations that ate into our work days and pushed aside sleep, we began to make some headway. I was able to understand that for Denzil, misplaced bread knives and unmade beds were harbingers of world collapse. Even though I thought this was silly, it was really no sillier than my adolescent-like refusal to hang up my coat simply because I'd been asked to. After careful explanation, Denzil was able to understand that examining and commenting on my every move twenty-four hours a day was going to make me insane. Understanding these things helped our real priorities snap back into perspective. We remembered why we thought this was a good idea in the first place.

# GROWING PAINS

Cara is fifteen, which means that I am stupid, have bad hair and can't dress. As Cara's comfort zone expands, mine contracts. She wants to play pool on Haight Street, I want to lock her in a tower until she's twenty-five. We've settled on letting her ride the bus home from school.

"Mom, you are so ridiculous. All my friends ride the bus," Cara whines as we scramble out of the house and into the car at 7:55 a.m.

"All I said was sit near the driver and don't talk to anybody, don't even make eye contact with anybody."

This is a whole new game for us and I'm reluctant to play it at all. The bus route through our old neighborhood ran through two sets of housing projects and would have dropped her three blocks from home. I've seen people get yanked from that bus and be beaten in the street. I watched a bus driver on that route plow into the back of a Buick on a sunny day. There was no way I was going to let Cara get on that bus. But our new neighborhood has a safer bus route that drops her off right in front of the house. This makes me feel slightly more confident that she'll make it home in one piece, but undercuts my excuse for not letting her ride the bus.

"You are so paranoid, Mom. It's not like the buses are filled with murderers and rapists."

"I know," I say. But I can't help remember that the last time Cara and I rode the bus a wild-eyed man sat behind us and whispered threats into my ear for five blocks, then followed us off the bus. We slipped into the skeezy corner store and examined the bruised fruit and dusty Cheez-It boxes until the shopkeeper chased him off.

We arrive at Cara's school and she ejects herself from the car as if it's a flaming plane. I roll down the window. "When are you going to be home?"

"If I don't get kidnapped or murdered, I should be home between six and seven, right after volleyball."

I spend an uneasy day spinning out T.V. movie-of-the-week scenarios: "Abduction—a simple bus ride turns into 24 hours of terror." "Cara—a childhood lost to the porn industry." I arrive home that evening as the sky is blazing pink and gold on one side of the house, and charcoal gray on the other.

At 5:30 I'm staring from our living room window at the bus stop across the street. I feel my heart pounding. My skin burns with prickles of heat. I'm embarrassed—technically, she isn't even due home yet and already I'm on the verge of hysteria.

By 6:00 the sky has turned black. I forgot how early it gets dark these days. A bus stops. Relief. She doesn't get off. Panic. I practice my yoga breathing exercises for about three seconds. They don't work. I'm not any calmer. I don't want to stand in the way of Cara's development, or her fun. I want her to get out there and explore what the

world has to offer. No, I don't. I don't want her to go anywhere or to explore anything, least of all anything fun. I
do, however, want her to come home, now.

"Would you get away from that window," Denzil
says. "She'll be here when she gets here."

"You just don't understand," I say in my weak
defense.

"Damn right I don't understand. She's fifteen years
old, she's smart and sensible and it's about time that kid
had a little independence."

I hate hearing those two words together, *kid* and
*independence*. If it were up to me we'd have started
counting backwards at her last birthday. I loathe the idea
of Cara growing up. As I approach the end of my tour of
duty I realize I have enough love and worry left over to
raise three more.

Denzil comes up behind me and gives me a hug.
"What were you doing at fifteen?"

"The usual fifteen-year-old stuff–bong hits on the
back of a flatbed pickup and forging my mom's signa-
ture."

"And you didn't have your mom hovering around,
did you?"

"No, but I was raised by wolves. And the point isn't
what I did, the point is, where the hell is Cara?"

Three buses have come and gone in the past fifteen
minutes and she still hasn't arrived. I force myself to stay
calm and assess the situation. The way I see it, there are
two possibilities–either she has been kidnapped and is
about to undergo surgery to have her organs removed for
black-market resale, or she has taken another bus route.

The other bus stop is four blocks away. I wander to
the kitchen to make some tea. I turn on the stove and
stare into the blue flame. Our neighborhood suddenly

becomes a dark playground. We live at ground zero of drug-addled rock 'n' roll history. Ashbury Street. Famous Ashbury Street, three blocks from the corner of Haight and Ashbury. The migrational point on the compass for music fans and aging hippies from all over the world. The Grateful Dead used to live in the purple house one block down, and the green one a block over, and the Victorian with the broken front steps half a block up. Janis Joplin bought Southern Comfort from the store on the corner. The first Jefferson Airplane album cover was shot on a porch two blocks away. Neil Young threw up in the azaleas across the street.

These days Haight Street is a gauntlet of shoeless runaways from Ohio, homeboys selling bud, girls with bangs and red lips shopping for platform shoes and furry jackets.

As I stare out at the night sky and sip my tea I remember a recent newspaper article citing our area as the city's landing pad for parolees, drug addicts and nut-cases being integrated back into society through halfway houses and rehab clinics. Troubling headlines tumble through my head like tennis shoes in a dryer. *Rehab Rampage*, and *Parolee Lures Unwitting Teen*.

I shout down the hall to Denzil, "I'm gonna run to the store to get some bread. I'll be back in a few minutes."

I run downstairs and very quietly open the garage door. I hop on my bike and ride to the bus stop four blocks away. I look at my watch. It's 6:14, I feel like a moron. I circle the block and wait for the next bus. Two Asian women get off. When Cara sees me combing the neighborhood she will accuse me of being all the things I am: paranoid, overprotective, and hysterical. The sky is black and the air biting cold; my body is hot and sticky. Two more buses come and go without delivering my daughter. I ride back home.

It's 6:30. I'd like to be furious, but she isn't actually even late yet. As I return to my perch at the window I remind myself that abject paranoia always overshadows intuition when it comes to my child. More times than I can count, I've been absolutely certain she's been run over or fallen off a cliff, or swept off the beach by a rogue wave. I've known it, I've felt it in my gut.

I run a bath because I believe warm water cures everything. As the tub fills, I pace from the kitchen to the front window three times. I remember the story of a fourteen-year-old being stabbed on the bus. "But she's fifteen," I say, as if there is a shelf date for bus stabbings. "She can take care of herself," I say.

Denzil stands in the bathroom doorway as I strip down and step into the tub. "What exactly are you afraid of?" he asks.

"You don't want to know," I moan.

I sink into the bath and let the hot water slip over me. I close my eyes and start designing missing person posters. I try to remember what she was last seen wearing. I calculate the reward. The phone rings. Denzil picks it up, talks for a moment, then hangs up. I hear his footsteps drawing toward the bathroom. I brace myself for the bad news. When Denzil comes into the bathroom I am standing bolt upright, dripping wet and naked. I'm trembling as my imagination runs wild. "They've found her," he'll say, "behind a liquor store, missing a kidney."

"That was Cara, she's at Melissa's," he says. "She didn't want to walk home from the bus stop alone in the dark. Asked if I'd come get her."

Late that night in bed I think that letting Cara grow up is proving much more difficult than raising her ever was. Aside from being concerned about her safety and welfare, boys, drugs, alcohol, and alien abduction, I'm concerned about myself. It's been fifteen years since I've made a decision that didn't take Cara into account. I'm not sure I know how to do it. I don't remember what freedom is, or what to do with it, and I doubt that marriage will change this.

I lie there watching the headlights from passing cars dance on the wall, feeling Denzil asleep beside me. I estimate the hours I've spent driving Cara to and from school, delivering her to orthodontist appointments, circus class, soccer games and birthday parties. I come up with roughly 6,000 hours. Then I calculate how many lunches I've made: 1,980. I try to make a mental list of all the things I will do instead but come up frighteningly blank. I never thought I'd be one of those mothers who has built her life around raising her children and doesn't know what to do with herself when it's over. But apparently I am. The same responsibilities I have, at times cursed under my breath have become intrinsic to my life, a definition of my time and space. I've grown fond of the relentless regime of parenting and I just want everything to slow down.

Raising Cara has allowed me to be the mother I wish I'd had, and seeing her grow up is the closest I'll ever get to a happy childhood. I'm not willing to toss that away for some junkie freak on the bus. I squirm up closer to Denzil and wonder if it's too late to have more children.

# THE PROPOSAL

The smell of burnt toast permeates the house. It wends its way down the long hallway and creeps into the bedrooms, the bathroom, the living room and office. Denzil and I run from opposite ends of the house to the kitchen where Cara is fishing two charcoal disks from our ancient toaster with a fork. "When are we going to get a new toaster?" Cara whines as she flings the blackened toast into the sink.

"You know," Denzil says, walking toward me and wrapping his arms around my waist, "sometimes people get toasters as wedding gifts." He kisses me on the neck.

"You guys are gross," Cara says, pulling a box of cereal from the cupboard.

"How 'bout it?" Denzil asks, giving me a squeeze.

I look at Cara through the smoky haze and think the last time I got married it was because I was pregnant, and even that was a better reason for getting married than needing a new toaster. I peel Denzil's hands off me.

"I hope that wasn't a marriage proposal, because if it

was, you'll need to do better than that. Something with a ring and a date."

"A ring and a date," I can hear my mother's voice cry out in my head. "Dr. Laura says don't move in with him until you have a ring and a date." Every conversation with my mother in the past six months has been peppered with advice from the radio talk show host Dr. Laura Schlessinger. I have visions of my mother causing traffic accidents as she takes notes for my benefit while merging lanes on the freeway.

"I'm pretty sure we're going to get married," I've told her, "or we wouldn't have moved in together."

"What makes you think he's any different?" she'd fire back. "He'll do what every other man on the planet does, he's going to put you off and put you off, take up what's left of your childbearing years, then walk away whenever he darn well pleases."

The best advice my mom ever gave me was to tear up the unflattering pictures of yourself when you pick up your photos from the photo shop. She's hardly someone I consult on matters of the heart.

"Mom," I'd interrupt, "I'm thirty-eight, my daughter is fifteen, my childbearing years barely exist anymore. As for walking away whenever he darn well pleases, one thing I've learned is there's not much I can do about that."

"Well, you tell Denzil you want a ring and a date, or you're going to move back out."

"Did you ever meet our last roommate?" I'd ask. "Did you ever actually see her bedroom? The entire floor was carpeted in food containers and dirty laundry, and she liked it that way. And the roommate before that, that big Texan guy, did you ever meet him?"

"He seemed like a very nice young man. I always

wondered why you never dated him. Lord knows you gave everyone else a go."

"He cleaned his guns in the garage, Mom."

"I'm tired of burnt toast," Cara says between bites of cereal.

"And you'd be willing to marry your mom off to get a new toaster?" Denzil says.

"If that's what it takes." Cara smiles, the same mischievous smile she's been smiling since she was three. The fact that she likes Denzil enough to joke like this is amazing to me. It's beautiful. This is the version of family I've been holding out for.

"A ring and a date, a ring and a date," Denzil chants.

"It's just that I want more of a story than our toaster broke, so we decided to get married," I explain.

"I'll work on it."

That evening, Denzil calls me into the living room. A full moon hangs in the night sky, visible through the semicircle of windows that look out over the street. Two small lamps with golden bulbs make the room glow like a Halloween pumpkin. Denzil sits me down on the chair across from the fireplace. He stands in front of me, nervously jangling the change in his pockets. A motorcycle rumbles past and the windows rattle. Without a word he produces a ring from his pocket, a small silver ring with two jade squares side by side on its rectangular top.

Denzil and I'd already had the diamond discussion. Part of me really *wanted* to want a big gaudy diamond engagement ring, something that would blind people from across the room at cocktail parties, but I couldn't actually picture one on my hand. I have utilitarian hands, the palms are callused from drumming, my nails are uneven and unpolished and usually stained with paint. A diamond would seem out of context.

"I want you to have this," he says, slipping the ring on my ring finger. "I bought it this afternoon, and if you don't like it we can get you another one, but I thought it was nice and it seemed like something you would like, and by the way, would you marry me?"

I respond with a series of choked squeaks and squeals, all of which mean yes. The difference between Denzil and nearly everyone else I've gone out with is that he gets me. He understands me. Some men have thought my jokes were distasteful and mean. One was perpetually disappointed that I didn't look like Susan Dey. An art collector I dated tried to get me to wear my hair up so I'd look like a Dallas socialite. Someone else told me I looked like a golfer's wife. My flaws were as many as the directions they came from. For some, my flaws have been insurmountable. Others have targeted me as good material that, with a little fine-tuning, could be a good catch. Denzil sees the same flaws everyone else has seen, but has the good grace to view them as attributes.

Denzil was the first man I dated who I didn't have to apologize to for my child's behavior. In fact, all indications were that Cara liked him. When we went to the beach she didn't sprinkle sand in his food, or break into finger-pointing laughter the moment he stumbled over a word or tripped on a crack in the sidewalk. She didn't pelt him with rubber bands when he came up the walkway to our flat. Granted, by the time Denzil came on board he had missed everything from the inconvenience of babyhood, the clumsy years of middle childhood, and the acerbic preteen years. Now, at fifteen, Cara was a happy and loving child. The teenage rebellion I'd been anticipating, preparing for, and steeling myself against had smoothed into a mild seething that didn't show itself often.

Somehow I had managed to meet a single man built for family life, living right here in the middle of San Francisco where any romantic combination is possible as long as it doesn't include a straight man over 30 who wants to get married and raise a family. I've found a needle in a haystack, and yes, of course I want to marry him.

I run down the hall to Cara's bedroom. She's sitting at her desk doing homework and listening to Bob Marley.

"Cara, look, we're getting married." I thrust out my hand to show her the ring.

"Good," she says, barely looking up from her homework. I'd have gotten the same level reaction if I'd told her we were going bowling. But I'm not bothered. I know if she objected her protests would be loud and vocal.

"Do you think you could draw something for the invitation?" I ask. "Something weddingy, flowers, bows, hearts, whatever."

"I guess so," Cara answers without looking up.

# LOCATION, LOCATION, LOCATION

The bed is strewn with bridal magazines. Ten pages into my first one it becomes clear that there are rules to this game, firm rules, and a well-honed industry ready to help you comply. By page thirty I feel like I used to feel at high school football games where I'd watch the other students feverishly jumping up and down, screaming and shouting like maniacs, all worked up over I didn't know what. I understood they were experiencing genuine excitement, but I didn't get it. I felt like I was missing the punch line to a very obvious joke. I flip through the magazine looking at cakes and rings and decorating ideas, I read a couple of advice columns, and again, I just don't get it.

"What sort of wedding do you want to have?" I ask Denzil, who is tucked into bed beside me reading Mary Shelley's *Frankenstein*.

"I don't care what sort of wedding we have," he says, "as long as we still want to get married after planning it. How about you, what sort of wedding do you want?"

I should have been prepared for this question, but I'm not.

"I haven't really thought about it," I say, and I'm not lying. I know plenty of women for whom a marriage proposal is nothing more than a signal to unveil the wedding plans they've been hatching since they were nine years old, but I am not one of them. In my personal catalogue of superstitions it seemed like bad luck to think about the details of a wedding before the decision of who exactly to marry was firmly anchored on the horizon.

As a child, I dreamt of being a cliff diver and being Cher. I never dreamt about being a bride. If marriage fantasies did manage to slip into my mind they always came to me in the same unflattering light as my visions of motherhood, which had me desperate and depressed, standing in a suburban park, thirty pounds overweight with a screaming kid on my hip. Motherhood has been nothing like this, but I still can't shake the vision.

Scanning my wedding memories, I realize that for the past several years every wedding I've attended has fallen just one side or the other of my own catastrophic heartbreak.

My older brother's wedding came on Halloween, just as I was in the thick of my divorce. I spent most of the reception crying in the bathroom. My mother got married the day after I was dumped by a Welsh submariner. Valium got me through the wedding, and helped me come to terms with the fact that I wouldn't be moving to a small Welsh coal-mining village anytime soon. I spent most of that wedding crying in the bathroom too. Malia, my friend of twenty years, got married on the heels of one of my particularly ugly versions of heartbreak, brought on by a boyfriend who hopped a plane to London while I was at the grocery store. Cutting the relationship short by a marriage and a lifetime and all the other reasons he'd sold his record and book collections and moved into my house halfway across the world.

"I haven't really enjoyed weddings much," I say distractedly.

I continue to thumb through page after page of perfect brides, coupled with perfect grooms, perfectly matched like collectors' sets of salt and pepper shakers. Diamonds, silverware, this season's headpieces, this season's veils, this season's dresses and dresses and dresses.

I tear out the two-page itemized list of wedding preparations with recommended lead times and a box to check off when the task is complete. Set date, secure location, decide on theme, decide on colors, mail "save the date" cards, choose bridesmaids, interview florists, interview D.J.s, interview photographers, shop for best man gift. I want to think that all of these tasks have some correlation to the development of our relationship. If we can decide on cake filling, then we can raise a family. If we agree on seating arrangements it'll be a breeze to decide if we'll eat dinner in the living room or at the kitchen table every night. Settling on an hors d'oeuvres selection is perfect practice for negotiating household finance issues. But I doubt it.

I naïvely thought we could just get married. It seemed like such a good idea to just get married. But now looking through these magazines, seeing what we're up against, the whole process seems a lot more complicated than I remember or anticipated.

"These magazines are filled with nothing but rules," I say. "Everything has its specific protocol. Right ways and wrong ways. How to word your invitations, how much you should spend on your bridesmaids' gifts, the right way to arrange seating for the reception, what to wear to your rehearsal dinner."

Rules have an intoxicating effect on Denzil and me, and rebellion on any scale comes easily for both of us. Given a rule to challenge, challenge we will.

"This is bullshit," I complain, tossing the magazine onto the floor and clicking off the light.

"Right," Denzil says, like an adamant four-year-old, "this is our wedding and we can do it any way we like."

"Yeah."

I wake up early on Sunday morning. From our bedroom window I can see the fog flooding over Sutro Tower and drowning half the city. I've gone from sound asleep to wide awake without passing through the half-awake but still dreaming stage, which has always been one of my favorite parts of the day.

Jessica's daunting monologue runs though my head again. I repeat it out loud, yanking Denzil from his slumber. *Now you have to think about the date, and the place, and your dress, and the ring, and your hair, and the music, the food, cake, guests, invitations.* A flush of anxiety races through me. I feel my face go cold and my stomach tighten. I'm reluctant to let a to-do list impinge on our romance and don't want to celebrate our union by spending the next six months shopping and organizing. I don't want the glitter and glamour of such a celebration to detract from the importance of what we are doing. I realize I want to *be* married more than I want to *get* married.

"Maybe we should just elope," I suggest.

"Is that what you really want?" Denzil asks sleepily.

"Not really," I admit. "You?"

Denzil props himself up on his pillow. "I keep thinking about something my mom said when I told her about the engagement. She said you don't want the wedding you remember to be the one you wish you could forget."

It takes me a minute to untangle the phrase. "Very poetic," I say. Then I remember the porch and the plastic flamingos, my mother's cackling laughter, and the burn on my forehead that took two months to heal. And I think about Denzil growing old with the memory of his first wedding overpowering that of his second.

"Okay," I say. "So the task at hand is to plan a wedding that will obliterate the memories of both our previous weddings."

"I'm not sure I like how that sounds," Denzil says, "but yeah, I guess so."

We stare out at the fog for a while longer.

"When do you want to get married?" Denzil asks.

"October," I answer. "It's the nicest month of the year here."

"Okay, October is good. How many people should we invite?" Denzil asks.

"I have no idea."

"Okay, should we have it indoors or outdoors?"

"Either."

"Do you want to get married in a church?"

"Not particularly."

"So basically we have no idea how we want to do this, except that we want to get married in October," Denzil says. "That's probably a good place to start."

In the span of one weekend Denzil and I transform into party planners. It seems clear from the stack of mind-numbing bridal magazines I spent last night poring over that before we can set the rest of our plans into motion we need a location for the wedding. A location will help determine the date, the guest list, the budget, the dress, the shoes.

I look through local bridal resource guides in the

bookstore for listings of mansions and wineries and dance halls. I call the San Francisco Parks and Recreation Department to get a list for public sites available for weddings. We clear our schedules one afternoon and head out on our first fact-finding mission.

After seven wrong turns and a quarter-mile trudge through wet grass, we find the Shakespeare Garden in Golden Gate Park.

"This place is nice," I say.

"If you don't mind your wedding hall being decorated with Mickey's Big Mouth bottles and french fry boxes," Denzil says.

He's right. Though the place is lovely at first glance, green and lush with ornate metalwork and a brick fireplace, it has all the markings of a city park: graffiti, trash, sleeping bags stuffed behind bushes.

"It could be cleaned up," I suggest.

"Is that what you want to be doing on your wedding day? You in a wedding dress slogging through the wet grass with a Hefty bag."

"I guess not."

We get back in the car and drive around the sprawling park until we find the Chain of Lakes wedding site, which appears to be a flat spot in the mud between two duck ponds.

"I'm not getting married there," I say firmly. Denzil insists on getting out for a closer examination. I insist on staying in the car.

We make our way across the park to check out the pagoda in the center of Stow Lake. "This is it," I squeal. "We get married in the pagoda, then make our getaway in a paddle boat with colored streamers and plastic bottles tied to the back." Denzil rolls his eyes.

While we drive through the Presidio on our way to

the nondenominational chapel at the top of a hill, I find myself haunted by thoughts of Denzil's first wedding. I know only a few things about it. I know that it was large and expensive and that people flew in from all over the country to be there. He and his first wife were married in a church I drive past nearly every day. I know they spent a full year planning the wedding, which made things all the more heartbreaking when it ended in an abysmal mess after only four months.

I am rocked by jealousy every time the subject of Denzil's previous marriage comes up. My ability to wallow in retroactive jealousy is one of my least attractive qualities. I'm torn between wanting to know everything about his previous wedding and wanting to know nothing.

There must be a road up to the chapel but we can't find it, so we park and hike to the top of the hill. The chapel is a Spanish-style building with thick white walls and lonely wooden pews. There's a grand piano and a conga drum on the altar. The faint smell of sandalwood incense lingers in the air. A huge vacant space looms above the altar where a crucifix once hung. The absence of the cross is so glaring that rather than creating a non-denominational feel, I'm led to fill in the void with a crucifix much larger and more macabre than anything that would have been there. I have no idea what goes on here but I start to imagine fairy queen hippie girls dancing in circles to the beat of congas, their floor-length skirts spinning into parachutes around them. Priests in long white robes chanting in some long-forgotten language as they walk slowly and deliberately up the aisle, carrying billowing trays of incense.

"I think this could work," Denzil says.

I think the chapel is creepy, but I don't say this. I

want to make some headway. I am practicing the subtle compromises and accommodations that I imagine it takes to create a happy, sustainable marriage. "It could work," I say in a sunshiny voice. "Some flowers, some guests, it would be lovely."

We find the office and quickly discover that the chapel is booked every weekend for the next eighteen months. Unless we want to get married on a Wednesday afternoon, our search isn't over yet.

Three days later Denzil and I have an appointment to see the Swedenborgian church. I've passed this church for years while taking Cara to and from school. I'd stop and visit when I had some time to kill or something that needed to be thought about in the deep calm of a church. I enjoy the sensation of stepping into a church, though I attribute it more to the architecture than to the presence of God.

When I pull up and park, Denzil is standing on the steps wiping a smudge off the stained-glass window with his handkerchief. He's dressed like someone who wasn't planning to leave the house, wearing a pair of dirty khakis, a plaid wool hat and a royal blue windbreaker. Denzil works in advertising, his work flies him to cities around the world, but when he isn't traveling he works at home and can go for days without stepping outside. I sit and watch him for a minute and think, is this really the guy I am about to marry? This strange man dressed like a blind golfer who's so concerned about the welfare of a church window?

Denzil gives me a disapproving look as I climb out of the car. My hair is tied in a scarf, I'm wearing paint-stained overalls and worn-out work boots. My original plan was to become a famous painter. Then I started writing, and I revised my plan to include famous author. I figured that while I was busy developing these careers I would take freelance work here and there to support Cara and myself. That way I wouldn't get trapped in a full-time job that would interfere with the creative process.

I was half-right. These jobs have rarely interfered with my creative process, but teetering on the brink of destitution has. My flashes of inspiration are often doused by waves of panic and foreboding. My nights have often been disturbed by wakeful hours of worry. The fear of getting locked into a mind-numbing career has been replaced by my fear of being locked out of my house by an angry landlord to whom I owe three months of rent. The reality is, between working odd jobs and the constant threat of financial ruin, I'm pleased if I can find the time to stretch a canvas or scratch a few ideas on a Post-it note.

Creativity is unpredictable by nature, stories swerve in unplanned directions, paintings end up purple instead of chartreuse. Sometimes the end result is miles better than your original vision, other times really great ideas can mutate into unsalvageable messes. I'm afraid this may be what has happened to my professional life.

So far I've managed to stay a few steps away from the cat food aisle by working an endless stream of odd jobs, some very odd. While writing my first novel, I worked at a needlepoint store painting custom needlepoint patterns of dogs and pansies for bored rich women. The day my first book was published, I was delivering plumbing parts to a fish restaurant. I wrote a screenplay while working as a sculptor's assistant, installing neon, cutting plastic, and grinding metal. While writing my second book, I worked as a waitress serving brunch to hungover couples on Sunday mornings. Over the years I've designed CD covers, bought hundreds of pieces of secondhand luggage for a sculpture project, photographed bands, made rubber casts of manhole covers, built architectural models, refinished furniture, designed backpacks, retarred a roof and made hats for the Pillsbury Dough Boy.

As I walk toward the church steps I look down at my hands. I've spent the morning painting a sign the size and shape of a '57 Chevy pickup that'll hang outside a café in Seattle. My hands are stained with black paint and I look like I've spent the morning changing spark plugs.

The church is nestled into a garden of redwood trees, grass and roses. The interior of the small church is redwood and a candle chandelier made of deer antlers hangs in the center of the room. The dark walls are lined with wrought-iron candleholders and capped with painted glass. A cross, made of thin, bundled sticks, hovers over the altar. A deep fireplace warms the back of the room.

The minister meets us in the church office. As we tour the church, I catch Denzil straightening out a picture on the wall. Am I really going to have to put up with this anal-retentive Good Samaritan who is worried about the angle at which a stranger's pictures hang? Denzil catches me chewing on the end of my sunglasses and I imagine he's having his own doubts.

"What is it you like about this church?" the minister asks as we stroll the church garden.

"The architecture, mostly," I answer. I know this is the wrong answer but it's also the truth.

My parents did my brothers and me what I consider

the great service of not introducing us to any sort of religion. My mother was raised a Jehovah's Witness and couldn't get away from it fast enough. My father was a sort of Catholic, but not enough of one to teach his children anything more than the Lord's Prayer. This lack of dogma meant that none of us had to spend any time recovering or nursing undue guilt. It also meant we didn't have a god to blame when things went wrong, or to pray to for things we wanted. It really hasn't been an issue for me until now, when having a religious affiliation would make finding a location for the wedding a lot easier.

The minister leads us to his office and opens a large desk calendar. "Our calendar is pretty full. What date were you looking for?"

"October 15th," Denzil says.

"Sorry, we're booked," the pastor says without the least trace of regret.

The following weekend we visit a small chapel we heard about through the Park Service The chapel was designed and built in the '70s, with avocado-green carpet to prove it. An orange vinyl chair with impossibly long armrests is fixed into a swivel base at the front of the room like it's a Christian Star Fleet command post. The stained-glass windows that flank either side of the small building are all translucent earth tones. A Cubist-style Last Supper made of tiny colored stones imbedded in glue and separated by black string outlines hangs above the entrance to the chapel.

"The chapel has been closed for the past ten years," the maintenance guy, who's taken a break from cleaning windows, tells us.

I'd have guessed fifteen.

"You could have a real nice wedding in here, string some white ribbon along the pews, get some bunches of flowers. We'll shampoo the carpet for you and we'll give you a good price."

Denzil and I make a noncommittal *hmmm* noise.

The maintenance guy leans a little closer and speaks in a confidential tone. "Truth is, so far we've only managed to book three funerals. A wedding might help turn the tide."

Denzil and I both make the *hmmm* noise again. The advantages of this place are obvious; it's available any time and it's practically free. The disadvantages are that it looks like it's been decorated from the close-out shelf of a Midwestern crafts store. The place is so terrible it's practically irresistible. I love it, but for all the wrong reasons.

I look at Denzil and nod enthusiastically. He looks at the maintenance guy. "We'll have to think about it for a little while. We'll get back to you."

When we get outside Denzil says, "You really want to get married in that dump?"

"Why not?"

"You just like it because it's strange."

"Considering our success so far, strange doesn't seem like such a bad deciding factor."

Denzil nestles his head into my shoulder and whispers a firm, "No," into my ear.

It's been a week since our last expedition. So far the places I like Denzil doesn't and the places we both like are booked for the next twelve months. After several more strikeouts there is only one place left on our list, the City Club.

I arrive at the polished lobby of the Pacific Stock

Exchange building begrudgingly. I'm not sure I want the symbolism of the stock market tied into our wedding. I step into the dark wood elevator and fix my lipstick on the way up to the tenth floor to meet Denzil. The elevator stops and after a heart-stopping pause, the door lurches open.

I am greeted by Denzil and Kristy, the City Club's chirpy catering director. I give Denzil a chilly kiss and shake Kristy's hand.

"It's so nice to meet you, Ms. Holm, and congratulations on your big news." Kristy gives me a knowing wink, which instantly relegates her to the "people I don't like" column of my mental ledger.

Kristy tells us the history of the City Club. It was built in 1928 as a private club for stockbrokers. She walks us into the main room, a cavernous space with twenty-foot ceilings, and two walls of windows looking out onto the downtown cityscape. The ceilings are made of copper with gorgeous art deco designs pressed into them. Kristy walks us from one corner to the next pointing out the elegant murals that illustrate dining in the four corners of the world. We leave the room and go back into the lobby, where she points out the elevator doors, which have thin layers of silver, bronze and brass illustrating the four winds and two hemispheres.

Kristy speaks with the calculated niceties of a charm school graduate, using both our names at every possible junction. Her sentences are peppered with *if you will*, and *I have to say*, and *vis-à-vis*. Phrases that are even more meaningless than they sound.

"If you will, Pamela and Denzil, the room is very elegant, vis-à-vis the traditional elegance of European art deco styling."

Kristy leads us up the grand red-carpeted staircase to

the eleventh floor. The open stairwell is dominated by a huge Diego Rivera mural. I am mesmerized. Kristy jabbers on about the rental policy, the menu packages, the liquor selection. The mural illustrates the industrial revolution, it's painted in lush earth tones and it takes up the entire wall and climbs up onto the ceiling with a beautiful image of a woman in perfect diving formation. I am awestruck. I want to climb into it. I want to stretch my body into a swan dive and fall into the sun. I want to be orange and red and gold. My discouragement starts to wane. My bad mood fades. I see myself descending the red-carpeted stairs, the train of my wedding dress clinging artfully to the steps. I see my friends and family holding tall, fluted champagne glasses. Swimming in my contrived fantasy makes me feel like a 1930s film star and I can't imagine under what circumstances I will ever have the opportunity to feel this way again.

I think about all the friends who listened to my endless sniveling and long-winded stories about my pantheon of bad boyfriends. I think about the chore of acting happy around my daughter when I wasn't. I think about the excitement my friends feigned when I met someone new, even though they knew it was just a matter of time before I'd be squeezing a weepy dinner invitation out of them. I think about Denzil's friends who have whispered to me how glad they are to see him happy. I think about the dreams Denzil and I whisper to each other in the middle of the night. I am swept away by an onslaught of previously dormant bridal fantasies: walking down the aisle in billows of white silk, Denzil looking dapper, a huge smile on his face. My friends laughing and crying and marveling in disbelief that such a thing could happen, that I am actually getting married.

I emerge from this daydream convinced that I don't

want to have my wedding at Star Fleet command, or the nondenominational-incense-conga chapel, or the church with the great architecture and a god who isn't on our guest list. I want a long white dress and uncomfortable shoes. I want to see my friends in evening gowns and dinner jackets. I want a big festive wedding, a true celebration with food and music and flowers and friends. The kind of wedding "encore brides" aren't suppose to think about.

"Are you still thinking of October 15th?" Kristy asks.

"Yeah," Denzil answers.

Kristy opens the leather-bound notebook she's been clutching throughout the tour.

"How lucky! The Rotary Club just canceled an awards ceremony booked for the 15th. It's all yours if you want it, Mr. Meyers and Ms. Holm."

Denzil sees me smiling.

"I could get married here," I say.

Denzil's face looks like a ringing cash register. He forces a weak smile and nods. "Okay."

# THE ENGAGEMENT DINNER
## — OR —
## DROP THE KNIFE AND
## STEP AWAY FROM THE CUTTING BOARD

"Let's have a party," Denzil suggests, "a dinner party to celebrate our engagement."

"A dinner party sounds great," I say, "as long as you're cooking."

I can see the recipe index flashing through Denzil's mind. He loves this sort of thing, an occasion, any occasion, to flex his culinary muscles. For Denzil, cooking is somewhere between a glamorous sport and an art, a way to create and share beauty. I approach food like a game show contestant, combining the ingredients at hand with little regard for recipes or taste, with the sole purpose of making something quickly. While Denzil has a knack for making everything he cooks taste good, everything I make tastes like it came from a recipe in the Boy

Scout handbook. Denzil cooks because he enjoys cooking. I cook because we get dizzy when we don't eat.

Denzil's cooking magazines and mail order catalogues clutter our countertops. Orders of stainless steel kitchen gadgetry arrive at our doorstep weekly. Our kitchen drawers overflow with an expanding collection of single-purpose instruments: stainless steel fish tweezers, a rubber-edged plastic tool for scraping chopped foods from the cutting board, a task I've always thought the palm of my hand quite capable of performing. Our cupboards house a fleet of culinary power tools: Cuisinarts, blenders, beaters, waffle irons and an industrial-sized mandoline for making paper-thin slices of potato, or your fingers, depending on who's using it. A collection of Calphalon pans decorates one wall of our kitchen. Suede potholders hang from brass hooks next to our Wolf stove. All this is wasted on me. The only cooking technique on my list of things to try is roasting a chicken under the hood of my car on a road trip.

Together, Denzil and I mull over the guest list, matching people like ingredients, aiming to create a dynamic combination with enough tension to make things interesting, but not so much as to ruin the dinner party. Over the next few days I make a series of phone calls trying to coordinate everyone's schedule while Denzil pours over cookbooks and *Gourmet* magazines. Again and again he busts into my office saying things like, "How do you feel about Etruscan?" and "Do you think squab for ten would be too much trouble?" Finally after days of deliberation and countless sample menus, he makes a decision. He calls it Bastardized Italian.

Next, Denzil creates a detailed shopping list and sets off on his grocery expedition, which takes upwards of two hours and several hundred dollars.

The cooking begins hours before our guests arrive. On a small piece of paper which he tapes to a cupboard he's drawn up a timeline, a plan of action: 6:40 start portobello mushroom mousse; 7:10 rub chicken with walnut oil and herbs de Provence, 8:45 sauté baby carrots; poach figs. The occasion and date of the meal is noted at the top of the paper, which he will later paste into a notebook for archival reference. Denzil does this sort of thing.

By the time our guests begin to arrive, the house smells delicious. The mingling scents of mushrooms, roast chicken and rosemary waft through the hallway, out the entry hall and onto the porch. Denzil has set the table with white linens and matching dinner plates, soup bowls and salad plates, water glasses and wineglasses and a stiff lineup of silverware. He has recruited Cara to calligraph menus, which are placed at either end of the table, while place cards spell out prearranged seating for our guests. I have stayed out of the way.

Our strange cross-section of friends have mixed seamlessly. Elise, a documentary filmmaker who is about to move to Hawaii to live in a treehouse sits at one end of the table. Next to Elise is Joe, an industrial designer who has to endure the *Goddamn it, Joe* curse whenever the round-handled knives he designed for Pottery Barn roll off the edge of our plates and onto the floor, as they do repeatedly during dinner. Stephanos, the lead singer of a Tom Jones tribute band, sits between Elise and Luchi, the Venezuelan beauty who talks like Ricky Ricardo and acts like Lucille Ball. On the other side of Luchi sits Nigel, an eccentric Englishman who runs an ad agency but can't drive a car. Next to Nigel sits Christine. Christine and Cara will be my two bridesmaids. Christine is large and lush and dressed in red leather pants and four-inch platform shoes that make her just over six feet tall. She's wearing a top with an image of a Hindu Goddess that is pulled tightly across her bust, distorting the Goddess' large eyes and stretching the mouth into an enormous smile. I have never once heard Christine make even the slightest reference to dieting. She moves through the world with a strength and confidence diet-supplement hawkers would tell you is impossible and it's beautiful to see. Cara sits between Christine and Jerry, Denzil's best man. Denzil asked Jerry to be his best man because he's his oldest friend in San Francisco, and someone I've never dated. Jerry is kind and soft-spoken, someone Denzil feels confident won't insist on dragging him to a strip club the night before the wedding.

Once everyone is settled at the table, Christine leaves briefly and returns with an enormous bottle of champagne. "I'd like to propose a toast," she says while peeling off the foil and undoing the wire from the top of the bottle. She works the cork with her fingers until it flies across the room and champagne erupts.

When everyone has a glass Christine raises hers and begins speaking. "The first time I met Denzil it was out in the desert and I painted him blue. When I met Pam she was also blue, but in more of an icky-boyfriend sort of way. Anyway, it's been a long time since I've seen either one of them blue, and I'd like to toast to them staying that way."

I met Christine through Matt, when he and I were on the verge of breaking up for the second or third time. In a relationship-salvaging measure Matt and I rented a house in Mexico for a week with a group of his friends. Christine was one of them. She has always maintained that Matt and I were the worst couple ever.

I've chosen Christine as my maid of honor because she is a good friend and someone who I suspect has never been nervous about anything. I've also chosen Cara because I really want her to be a part of the ceremony, and she looks good in anything so her presence will enhance the wedding party pictures considerably.

"What do you think about all this wedding stuff?" Jerry asks Cara.

"It's fine."

"Fine?" Christine repeats.

"Yeah, it's good, whatever."

"What do you think of Denzil?" Christine asks.

"He's kind of annoying, but he's cool, I guess."

"What's annoying about him?" Jerry asks.

Christine, Cara and Jerry look over at Denzil, who has fastened the wire top from the champagne bottle around the tip of his nose. He looks like the Tin Man.

"Never mind," Jerry says.

Throughout the meal, the conversation is dominated by talk of food. Politics, gossip, divorce, and job complaints are all eclipsed by questions about spice combinations and how long the radicchio was steamed before it was blah, blah, blah. Denzil answers these questions as if he were giving the keynote address at the Culinary Academy. People ask questions about my meals, too, but they're more along the lines of "are these black things chicken or beans?" and "how *did* you get the soup to taste this way?"

I've watched Denzil in this role before, the rooster strut of the home chef, the chest-pounding antics of someone who romanticizes kitchen drudgery, but now with marriage looming on the horizon, the stakes seem higher. I realize that by marrying the Galloping Gourmet this sort of dinnertime glad-handing is about to become an integral part of my social life.

What bothers me isn't the complicated food or the care that goes into preparing it, or even the attention that is showered on Denzil all through dinner. To be bothered by these things would imply deep character flaws, a soul ridden with childish jealousy. No, what really bothers me is that my fiancée has raised the bar of cooking at our house, and raised it way above my head. Now that Cara's culinary tastes have been corrupted and she has developed snobbish cravings for goat cheese and lentil salad, spit-roasted squab with anchovy-olive butter, she gets nervous when she sees me milling around the kitchen at dinnertime.

"Are you cooking tonight?" she'll ask anxiously.

In the old days it was much easier to pass off questionable dishes: fried potatoes with a side of carrot sticks and peanut butter; grilled cheese sandwiches and frozen peas; turkey hot dogs and raspberry yogurt. Left to my own devices, I was free to plumb the depths of bad cooking without interference, complaint or the need for explanation. She didn't know the difference.

Now, with the advent of real cooking in our house, my unquestioned parental authority is being questioned.

"Is that really what lasagna is suppose to look like?" and "Mom, bologna and cream cheese rolled up in white bread is not sushi."

Denzil brings a steaming dish of coq au vin to the table and the room erupts into applause. "Anyone can follow a recipe," I mumble quietly, but then I remember the chicken gumbo that came out solid and made everything in the coat closet smell like hot oil for six months.

The silence of concentrated eating overtakes the congratulatory murmur at the table. I remind myself that things could certainly be worse. I remember the boyfriend who had mastered cooking boil-in-the-bag white rice, but little else. And another who thought meatloaf was manna, and yet another who made a sickening dish he called mucky-muck that consisted of cream of mushroom soup, egg noodles and canned chicken.

While Denzil has embraced food preparation as a creative act, I blame my own creative endeavors for my culinary defeat. Some of my best writing has gone hand in hand with my worst cooking. When the words are flowing I am willing to sacrifice an entire meal to tap out a couple of clever lines. To make things worse, cooking inspires me to write. I run back and forth between the kitchen and my desk, where I furiously take notes, then back to the kitchen to scrape dinner off the bottom of the pan.

During creatively fertile times, the kitchen becomes a dangerous place for me. Brown crescent-shaped scars branded into my wrists and forearms mark the places where imagination and hot cookware have collided. Unfortunately, these marks look more like clumsy suicide attempts than battle scars of inspiration.

Creative aspirations aside, another reason for the disparity in cooking styles at our house is simple: Denzil has never encountered the humdrum relentlessness of the everyday cooking world. The fifteen years I've spent making breakfasts, packing lunches and burning dinners for Cara, he has spent developing his career, dining out and occasionally treating his friends to meals that require only slightly less work than an Indian wedding feast.

Denzil has an enviable lifestyle. When he works, he works hard—airports, hotels, meetings, staying up all night preparing reports, etc. When he's not working he lives like a sixteen-year-old on summer vacation. He'll sleep until 10 o'clock, read the paper till noon, play drums for a few hours, ride his bike, take a nap, then stay up till 2 a.m. composing music.

Denzil enjoys family life, but he's adjusting to it at his own pace. Some mornings he will leap out of bed and offer to drive Cara to school, but he wouldn't think to plan his errands so he can swing past the school at dismissal time. He'll assemble amazing five-course meals, but wouldn't dream of thinking ahead to plan for dinner that night. But still, I consider myself extremely lucky. No one else has ever offered to drive Cara to school before.

At the end of the meal we lean with elbows on the freshly stained tablecloth drinking coffee and sipping single malt whisky to the soundtrack of, "Denzil, that was the best meal I've ever had," and "I'll have to get that recipe from you." I've had enough. I want to stand on the chair and tell them that Denzil's great with a cookbook but couldn't fly by the seat of his pants with a propeller attached to his ass. I want to tell them about Denzil's one bad meal. A meal so monumentally bad that no matter how many five-star dinners he serves up, he'll never live down the vinegar-pomegranate molasses-vegetable stir-fry. But that would be rude and they'd all know that I was just jealous. Anyway, if I dared say anything disparaging about Denzil my own friends would defend him. They adore Denzil. I smile and sip whiskey and wait for our guests to get sleepy.

# THE DRESS

Wearing my mother's wedding dress is out of the question, though if she still had it, it would probably fit me perfectly. I grew up looking at a black-and-white picture of my parents' courthouse wedding. My mother is seated in front of a desk, pen in hand, about to sign the marriage certificate. She's wearing a beautifully tailored suit that she made herself, her hair is pinned back neatly, and she's looking straight into the camera. My father stands to one side of the desk. He's wearing a black suit and has his hair combed into a pompadour. The looks on their faces are closer to bewilderment than happiness, exactly.

I'm not sure what sort of a dress I want to wear. I have no idea how long this process is going to take, or how much I can expect to spend. I crack open the phone book. On the second page I recognize the name Brenda Forman as the woman from my Brazilian dance class who designs our costumes for the annual Carnival parade. Last year's costumes were blue and white with fringe and sequins and bands of Mylar streamers that hung from our wrists and knees. We wore felt headdresses with eight-inch foamcore cutouts of glittery sea creatures. Together the eighty-plus dancers were supposed to look like the ocean; instead we looked like a street full of bouilla-baisse, and individually we looked like Dallas Cowboy cheerleaders with crustaceans on our heads. I'd heard Brenda designs beautiful wedding dresses, but that's a lit-tle hard for me to believe. I skip down the page to the advertisement for *Love Salon, Judith Love, Wedding Dress Designer.* How can I resist a place called *Love Salon?* I call and set up an appointment for the next day.

The Love Salon is run out of the designer's Pacific Heights home. When I knock Judith opens the door and introduces herself with a firm handshake. She is in her mid-fifties, and dressed in the drapy black clothes of the arty and rich. As we climb the stairs, Judith asks, "Any idea what kind of a dress you're looking for?"

"Something simple," I say.

Judith laughs a deep and potentially insulting laugh. "That's what every bride on the planet says."

She leads me across the room to a rack of dresses. Some are white, some off-white, a couple are a pale tea-stained brown. They are all silk. None are simple. I choose a beaded ivory-colored dress with an empire waist, a low back and a straight skirt that extends all the way to the floor. The weight of the beads pulls the dress downward, making it long and thin, as if it were designed for a nine-foot-tall anorexic bride. I think about Tony, a drag queen I knew when I was a teenager, who taught me to walk in high heels, and told me that if I ever had the chance to try on a beaded dress, I just *had* to do it. I lift the heavy dress off the rack and hand it to Judith. I choose a second dress. This one has thin straps, a low waist and several layers of sheer silk that make up the skirt. Judith leads me to the dressing room and orders me to strip down to my underwear. She wraps a measuring tape around my bust, then waist and hips.

"You're lucky," she says, "you're a size 4. That's the size of all our wedding dress samples."

"What happens if you're not a size 4?" I ask.

"Then we use our imaginations."

Judith dresses me like a doll, pulling the first dress over my head and buttoning the twenty tiny buttons that climb up over the curve of my lower back.

"All my dresses are sewn in Paris," she says. "No one on this continent can sew like the Parisians."

I silently mouth the words, "I'm having my dress made in Paris," just to see how it feels. I think the luxury of being able to utter this phrase in public has to be worth something. Probably more than I want to spend.

The dress fits me perfectly, except for the bust, which is a little too large. Judith shoves a pair of padded disks down the front of the dress. "You can wear these, it'll look better in the photos anyway."

"Can't those Parisians just make the dress fit?"

"They can, but it'll be an extra $250 to alter the pattern to fit you."

"So there's a $250 penalty for being flat-chested," I say.

"We like to call it an alteration fee," Judith says. "What size shoes do you wear?"

"Seven-and-a-half, eight."

Judith disappears out of the dressing room. I look down at the dress and notice that, through the silk and the glistening beads, it is curiously mangy. Filthy, in fact, as if grubby six-year-olds have been playing dress-up in it. There's a mosaic of faint multicolored lipstick smudges around the neckline. Tiny drool marks and coffee stains map a constellation down the front. The bottom of the dress is black from dirt. I go from feeling like a movie star to feeling like a character actress in a creature feature. The hysterical bride running through the foggy swamp, tree branches dripping with Spanish moss, the howl of hounds in the distance as I'm being chased through the bayou by the swamp monster. I look in the mirror and slide one strap off my shoulder and hunch over. I contort my face into an expression of zombie terror and lurch through the dressing room with my arms flailing out in front of me. When I look up, Judith is standing at the door, holding a pair of satin pumps. "Everything all right?" she asks.

"Fine," I answer. I slip the shoes on, lift the bottom of the dress up in one hand, and follow her back into the front room.

Judith positions me in front of a mirror, a magical mirror that somehow tosses back a reflection with no imperfections. In fact, nothing could dull the glow. The neck of the dress is cut in a wide scoop, the thin sleeves cap the edge of my shoulders. The dress hangs like a dream. The beaded fabric feels comforting and heavy. It clings to me like a full-body hug. I feel like a mermaid with a beaded fish tail, and I think Tony knew what he was talking about.

When I look down and smooth the dress across my hips, I see the stains and the grime and instantly want to wash my hands. I turn slightly and look back at my reflection, only this time all I can see is the bayou, the moss-draped trees, Swamp Thing gaining on me. "This is very beautiful," I say, "but I don't think it's the right one."

Judith gathers up the bottom of the dress and follows me back to the dressing room. She undoes the twenty tiny buttons and pulls the dress over my head. In the mirror I see myself dressed in nothing but worn satin shoes and underwear that doesn't match, white cotton panties and a charcoal gray bra. My skin looks pale and lumpy. I may be a size 4 but my body is still unruly, bulging in all the wrong places, concave in others. I've never felt less glamorous. While I'm busy cataloging my physical faults, Judith hangs up the beaded dress and takes the second dress off its hanger and threads it over my head and through my arms. This one is slightly cleaner, though it still has lipstick stains around the neckline. "I designed this one for my daughter's wedding," Judith says as she buttons up the back and pulls at the sheer silk underskirts. Again she shoves the falsies down the front of the dress.

When we go back to the front room the sun has shifted just enough to filter through the trees and create a golden glow in the room. I stand in front of the mirror and I am transformed. I am no longer someone who is getting married, I am a bride. Billows of silk and satin, yards of lace, and dozens of tiny hooks down the small of my back. Judith clips a long veil to the back of my head and lets it tumble to the floor. I nearly burst into tears. I look as if I've escaped from a Renaissance painting. I am Audrey Hepburn. I am Grace Kelly and Princess Diana. I am the Barbie Dream Bride. And through all this, as my mind skips from ancient times to romance paperbacks, I marvel at my normalcy. I'm amazed at my reaction. My rebellion against white-bread America comes to a screeching halt. So much for casting off rules and tradition, I've been seduced with frightening ease into the white wedding I didn't think I wanted. I stare at the halo of gauze that catches the light streaming through the windows. I study the ivory dress that rides the curve of my waist. I watch the layers of thin silk clinging to my thighs then fall to the floor. My longstanding vision of myself as nonconformist fades away, and I am caught off-guard with the truth, that I am just another middle-class white girl who wants to be a princess.

"How do you like it?" Judith asks.

"It's beautiful," I choke out. I really, really, really don't want to break the spell, but I know I have to. "How much is the dress?"

"Wait," she says, "you've got to see it with a necklace." She walks across the room and pulls a wispy choker from a glass cabinet. She fastens the necklace, which appears to be made of fishing line and a small handful of beads, around my neck. I say *hmmm*. The necklace is dreadful, but not so dreadful as to overshadow the radiance of the perfect dress and veil. Judith stands back and admires me like a cake she's just decorated. "This dress was made for you," she says, dragging the words out into a sugary declaration.

"How much is all this?" I ask again.

"The dress is $4,000."

I don't flinch. Somehow, in this context, with the golden light and the yards of silk and the Parisian hand-stitched detail and Judith in her heavy jewelry and rhinestone-studded eyeglasses, here in my romantic stupor, in this dress-up princess world, this price makes perfect sense.

"And the veil?"

"The veil is $400, but remember there are all sorts of things you can do with it after the wedding," Judith says, "use it as a tablecloth, for instance." I make a mental note to try on my tablecloths when I get home. "And the choker, well, it's not made with real gemstones, so it's only $900."

I reluctantly change back into my street clothes.

Judith writes the price of the dress, veil, and choker on the back of her business card. "If you want this dress by October 15th, you'll have to make up your mind by Monday."

I'm ready to say yes. Yes, yes, yes, I want the dress. I don't care how much it costs, money is no object, this is for my wedding day, this is something I'll do only once, not counting the last time. I want to live in the dress, I want to wear it home right now. I want the glass slippers that go with it, and a coach pulled by enchanted mice. But I force myself to say, "I need to think about it."

When I climb into my old Saab, the spell is broken. I paid half as much for my car as I am tempted to spend on a dress. A dress I will wear for a maximum of eight hours. That's $500 an hour, $8.33 per minute. I could be gilded for less.

I think about the hand-to-mouth existence I've had these past several years. I think about the calls from Cara's school demanding I pay the outstanding tuition bill before she can return to class. I think about the money I borrowed from my father, my ex-husband and three different friends, and eventually paid back. I remember the cop who pulled me over then had my car towed because the registration had been expired for eight months and I owed $300 in parking tickets. The PG&E notice stapled to the garage informing me and all my neighbors that my power would be cut off in 24 hours unless I came up with $340. The dinner party that was interrupted by a call from a collection agency, which I tried to make sound like a conversation with a friend. I think about the $5,000 advance I got for my first book, and the year it took to write it, and the six months it took to rewrite it. Then I think about the dress, and spending $4,000 seems beyond unreasonable.

On the way home, I remember the discount bridal store I always pass when I'm headed to the freeway; it's sandwiched between an auto repair shop and a place that sells silk flowers. If you park anywhere in that neighborhood for more than twenty minutes, you return to your car with a purple flyer tucked under your windshield wiper trying to lure you to a sale at Discount Bridal.

The store is huge, with dirty carpets and harsh fluorescent light. It's jammed with rows and rows of snow-white and ivory gowns hanging in plastic on metal racks. When I enter, there are four saleswomen standing around the counter at the front of the store. No one makes eye contact with me. I choose a couple of styles that seem promising. I lug the gowns to the dressing area in the back of the store. The room is stark with mirrors on three sides. Half a dozen anxious women are squeezing themselves into lacy gowns.

I find a vacant corner, strip down to my underwear and release the first dress from its plastic sheath. I climb into it and thread my arms through the long lace sleeves. I reach behind me and slide the zipper up as far as I can reach. The neck is low and scalloped; the bust of the dress retains its shape, which is nothing like the shape of my own bust. The dress is tight around my waist, then flares out into a billowy skirt made of several layers of satin and tulle. I back up from the mirror to get the full effect. I look like the crocheted doll that sits on the extra roll of toilet paper in my aunt's bathroom. I fish the price tag out of one of the lace sleeves, $300. I can't help but think it is way overpriced.

I look around at the women wiggling thighs, hips, torsos and breasts into the confines of these satin cocoons. Their flesh pressed up against the fabric, anxiety leaking out of their pores, staining the cloth with excitement and disappointment and I realize I don't want to be married in a dress that has been worn by anyone else, ever. As I peel off the gown I understand that a wedding dress is sacred clothing. A dress that takes you from one life to the next. I see the dress as a symbolic purification, a launching pad into a happy future.

I leave the store discouraged and confused. I am ready to call my acupuncturist's Guatemalan cleaning woman/seamstress. I picture acres of white crinoline, six-inch bows and scalloped lace sleeves. I don't care if I end up looking like a giant Latina toddler.

# THE GUESTS

When the kettle starts to scream Denzil turns off the burner and opens the cupboard. An avalanche of tea boxes slides out onto the counter and tumbles onto the floor.

"Sorry," I say sheepishly as I reach around him and pull two teacups out of the cupboard. I feel a twinge of guilt because the last three times I've made tea the same tea box eruption has taken place. All three times I crammed the boxes haphazardly back into the cupboard and went about my business.

I brace myself for a reprimand. I am ready with a defensive sneer, with eyes poised to roll skyward. My defense chatters away in my head: "Since when are the cupboards my responsibility?" But Denzil still doesn't say anything. He simply bends down and picks up the errant boxes of tea, tosses them back into the cupboard and closes the door quickly. He doesn't freak out, doesn't complain, doesn't take the opportunity to grudgingly reorganize the cupboard. Seeing this gives me a secret thrill. I am pleased that with all the amendments I have painstakingly made to my own behavior–towels, laundry, toothpaste caps–Denzil is making adjustments that reflect my values.

I fill our cups with steaming water and carry the tea to the dining room table, which is littered with paper and pens and address books. We've set aside the morning to finalize our guest list.

"How many do you have?" I ask.

Denzil taps his pen down the side of a lengthy column. "Ninety-eight," he answers.

"Jesus, ninety-eight, I don't think I even know that many people," I bark.

"How many do you have?"

I count my list. "Oh, eighty-two."

"That's a hundred and eighty people. No way," Denzil says, "that's ridiculous."

"Right," I say.

We take a minute to scrutinize our own lists. I lop off my aunts, uncles and cousins from my dad's side of the family in Canada. They may be offended, but they probably won't think any worse of me than they do already. My father, my brothers and I are all black sheep in the eyes of that side of the family. My father is the only one of his siblings who is divorced. I'm a divorced single mom, my brother Cameron's life is always in some sort of messy disrepair–jail, rehab, boyfriend troubles, whatever, which leaves my older brother, Greg, as the respectable one, and the day that Greg is the respectable one, we are all in trouble.

I watch the steam from my teacup draw smoky spirals in the air and scan my list again. This time I cut out the friends I haven't talked to in a few years, and the family friends I probably ought to invite. I leave Janie, my never-once-bought-food, slept-with-all-my-friends, nightmare ex-roommate, on the list because in spite of this I still like her.

After ten minutes my list has dropped from eighty-two to seventy. Denzil's has dropped from ninety-eight to eighty-nine. Still too many.

After scrutinizing our own lists we scrutinize each other's.

"Who's Bunny Wellington?" I ask Denzil.

"An old friend."

"Did you date her?"

"Not really," he says. I reach across the table and draw a line through her name with a red pen.

"Well, who's Morris?"

"A really good friend," I answer.

"Why does it say 'find' next to his name?"

"He moved a couple of years ago, never got his new number."

Denzil reaches across the table and says goodbye to Morris with the same red pen.

We try to devise a strategic rating system, but petty jealousy seems to be the standing factor. "You're not really planning on inviting her," I say as I grab the pen and draw a firm line through Marion Mitchell's name. Marion is one of Denzil's exes. Anything I deem distasteful—shag haircuts, elastic waistbands and bunchy sweaters, Sheryl Crow songs and teddy bears in rear windows—I automatically assign as a characteristic of Marion's—this woman I have never met (but know the subtleties of her bad taste oh-so-well). As far as I'm concerned, these negative attributes make up her entirety. I have no room for the truth, no room for pleasant or even realistic traits to counterbalance the facts as I see them. Actually, this system works best when there are no actual facts to conflict with my blind assumptions.

At moments of deep reflection, or even casual viewing from the corner of my eye, I can see that this game is a pathetic ploy to make myself feel better, more deserving of Denzil's love. It helps me establish a base of security, to strengthen my fortress, i.e., He'd never leave me for a woman who dresses in plaid stretch pants and T-shirts from Great America.

This behavior isn't inspired by Denzil or this particular ex. She is just the latest in a long line of badly dressed, lisping, pockmarked creations of mine. I dislike ex-girlfriends on principle. I dislike ex-wives even more. It's really nothing personal.

"That's hardly fair," Denzil says, "considering two of your ex-boyfriends are on your list."

"So?" I reply. "The way I feel about my own exes has no bearing on how I feel about yours."

I know this is unfair, but I have a large extended family made up almost entirely of my ex-boyfriends and their current spouses and children. If the climate is right, once the breakup has commenced and disgruntled parties have forgotten the messy details, after both parties have plowed through a couple of failed rebound stints, and one or the other has ended up with their rightful companion, it's easy to be friends. Not let's-go-to-lunch friends, but friends you call in emergencies, when water pipes break or you can't find your kids, or your keys, or you need to borrow $800.

"Okay," I relent, "I'm getting married, for God's sake, it's time to get over this crap. If you want Marion to be there, she should be." I write Marion's name back on Denzil's list. Denzil crosses it off again and kisses my cheek.

When we do a recount, the list is still far too long.

We start trading people like baseball cards. "Tell you what," I say, "you let go of Ronnie from high school in New Jersey, and I'll let go of rock star Michael in L.A. who I haven't talked to in three years." We do this for a while, wiping out great swathes of each other's pasts with red pen strokes, until we come up with a mutually agreed-upon list.

After all the careful chipping and filing, our combined list has a total of 120 guests. We're hoping that 20 of them can't make it.

We start to laboriously hand-address the invitations. The invitations are five inches square, printed on white paper with raised black ink and Cara's beautifully rendered image of a toaster with plumes of black smoke billowing out the top.

## THE DRESS SAGA, PART TWO

"What are you going to wear?" I ask Denzil while search-ing the phone book for an alternative to the $4,000 birds-singing-heavens-opening-up gown and the $300 toilet-roll-warmer dress.

"I thought I'd wear my tux," he answers.

"A tux. It's so damn easy," I say. "I spend a month looking for a dress and you're just going to open your closet."

I know this is the same tuxedo he wore to his first wedding, but I am determined not to address the issue directly. Because my feelings are hurt, and because I feel a little stupid and petty and immature, I've decided to fall back on my habit of dropping cynical hints until Denzil either gets the point or gets so frustrated that he finally asks me exactly what the point is.

I see an ad for a shop called *Dark Garden - Custom Corsetry and Wedding Gowns*. I make an appointment for the next day.

Dark Garden is on an alley in a neighborhood that

has taken stabs at gentrification, but nothing that's stuck. The store is lush with green carpeting and antique armoires. Dresses made of velvet and lace hang from racks. Bustiers and matching garter belts hang from another. A row of 1940s nightgowns made of coral-colored satin hangs against one wall. A salesgirl with maroon lips and dark hair approaches me. She's wearing a long black lace dress that fits like a tattoo and an expression that suggests a smile might kill her. I'm wearing an orange top and red pants. I look like a paint spill next to this dour display of glamour. "I'm Pamela," I say; "I have an appointment at 3."

"Glad you could come," the woman says, extending a pale hand. "I'm Violet."

Violet leads me across the store to a red velvet couch and hands me a photo album. "Our dresses start around $1,500," she says. "They go up from there." This seems reasonable—expensive, but not disgustingly so.

When Violet glides away to help another customer I open the book. A collection of slightly blurry brides stare back at me. Brides under trees, brides in front of Gothic churches with gargoyles skulking in the background, brides on stormy beaches. Ghoulish-looking women in corset tops and gathered skirts standing arm and arm with their spooky looking husbands. Medieval maidens wearing heavy brocades that make them look as if they've been upholstered. One heavy-set bride looks like her breasts are plotting a desperate escape from her bustier.

As I politely coo over the photos of strange brides, I'm distracted by a photograph that hangs on the wall above the cash register. A woman in a tightly laced patent-leather corset and thigh-high stockings is menacingly holding a leash, a stiletto heel pressed into the bare back of a man on his knees. A man wearing black leather hot pants and a spiked dog collar, to which the other end of the leash is attached. It's all starting to add up. Another photo hangs a few yards away: a man in blue eye shadow, a tight leather dress and thigh boots. The glass case below the cash register is filled with glinting metal bracelets, fur-lined handcuffs and mysterious hardware. The photos and the hardware startle me, but my reaction startles me more. I'm open-minded. I live in San Francisco. Nothing shocks me. My daughter and I can spot drag queens at fifty paces. Yet sitting on this red velvet couch, with the bondage photos, the vixen salesgirl, the strange brides, I suddenly feel like a Midwestern schoolmarm and all I can think is that I want to get out of here.

As I turn my attention back to the book in my lap, a dark-haired woman in a white three-quarter-length gown stares out at me with a pleading look, silently begging me to loosen her dress, which is cinched at the waist like a wasp.

Until now, all the bridal albums I've looked at while shopping for a dress have been filled with images of women who look like they ought to be named Buffy—perfect blonde debutantes marrying stockbrokers and accountants. I'm happy to see I'm not the only non-Buffy headed for the altar, but the photos of these brides are not tempting me toward any of these gowns. I'm reluctant to step into my new life dressed for dinner with King Arthur, or a peep show.

Once again, I postpone the dress search. I am not only hampered by my lack of interest in anything I have seen so far, except the $4,000 gown, but by my busy mind. I start to obsess about what Denzil's ex-wife got married in. Did it cost more or less than what I'm planning to spend? Where did she buy her dress? And most disturbingly, as wildly coincidental as it would be, what if I end up with the same dress? I picture Denzil seeing me for the first time as I walk down the aisle, his face going pale, the urge to bolt washing over him. I see his mother and sister in the front row with horrified expressions. Denzil's old friends snickering in the crowd. I try to push these thoughts from my head. I don't want to ask him what she wore, because I don't really want to know. For lack of any real information I decide to picture her in burlap. Floor-length burlap. It helps, a little.

When I resume my search I go to Rista Rose, a tiny boutique in North Beach that Jessica has recommended. The place is sunny and mirrored and run by two young women who have the disheveled look of art students, which automatically makes me feel at home. I immediately find ten dresses I love. Maybe I'm just learning how to shop, what to look for. Or maybe these dresses are really as beautiful as I think they are. Every dress I try on fits. The designer, who is perched behind the glass counter at the front of the store, looks up from her paperwork and smiles the first two times I step out of the dressing room. The third time I emerge from the dressing room she is sitting in the white leather chair across from the mirror, grinning proudly.

I narrow the selection down to three. Two days later I return with reinforcements—Luchi and Christine. I try on the three contending dresses.

"That is so beautiful," Luchi says when I come out of the dressing room in my favorite of the three. Tears well up in her eyes and my heart sinks. I know this must be difficult for Luchi, who is in the midst of a divorce. She's managed to funnel most of her pain into mountain biking. When she was married, she and her husband would go riding every weekend. He'd push her on difficult trails she thought were far beyond her ability. It wasn't until they split up and she started riding with other bikers that she found out she was actually really good. Her new friends encouraged her to start racing. She came in second place in her first race.

The thought of divorce is like a splash of cold water. As haphazardly as I entered into the marriage with Gary, getting out of it left me with a deep sense of failure. I draped dark fabric on the windows to block out the sun. I couldn't sleep or eat. And the memory of it all can never be far enough away.

The dress we choose is ivory, it has long mesh sleeves that cling to my arms; the shoulders and elbows are cut out, revealing triangles of skin. The back is open in a wide circle. Tiny buttons extend down the last six inches of my spine. The neck is square and tight across my bust. The skirt is bias-cut, so it falls to the floor and clings to my hips and thighs, outlining my muscles and fleshy curves and making me grateful for my samba classes. I feel more beautiful than I have ever felt. I swear I hear angels singing.

The dress is expensive, but only half as much as the one I was about to buy a couple of weeks ago. The price still freaks me out. I feel irresponsible and frivolous, bourgeois. When I get home I consider canceling the order. Instead, I spend the next two days doodling pictures of the dress like a lovesick teenager.

# R.S.V.P.

Within days of sending out the invitations we start to get calls, lots of calls. The messages range from poetically cryptic ("The only thing that would keep us from coming to your wedding is not knowing what time it starts") to blunt ("You forgot to put the time on the invitations, losers").

Over the next couple of days I call everyone on our guest list. "The wedding is at 2 o'clock, please make a note on your invitation, the graphic designer left it off." I don't mention that I was the graphic designer.

The response card from Denzil's mom comes back to us addressed to Mr. and Mrs. Denzil Meyers. I know she means this in the best way possible, but I find it strangely demeaning. It implies that my entire identity is about to be swallowed up by Mr. Denzil Meyers, deleting my first name in the process and leaving me with the moniker of some long-forgotten elementary school teacher.

I've decided not to change my name. After my first marriage I hyphenated my name, but only sometimes, and could never really decide whether Gary's long Greek name came first or second. Consequently I was Holm-Kritikos some places, Kritikos-Holm in others, then just Holm, or just Kritikos. I never knew where I was who. Consequently, doctors, dentists and school administrators could never find my charts. By the time I decided to be Pamela Holm-Kritikos, I was getting divorced.

Response cards start to roll in, many with mysterious interlopers attached. Invitations addressed to one yield responses for two. Names we've never heard before are scrawled on the backs of the cards. It seems a number of our single friends have suddenly coupled up and wouldn't dream of leaving their newly beloved alone for five hours on a Sunday afternoon.

This goes on for weeks. Every day we are delivered another installment of the guest list drama. We lie awake at night amending our tally and refiguring the dollar amounts. We're torn between the fear of financial ruin and being flattered by our sudden popularity.

At first we are understanding, we are polite and unwilling to be offensive. But the scales are tipped when we find out that three of our friends have yet to R.S.V.P. because they can't decide whom to bring as dates. At the risk of hurting their feelings, we decide to pre-empt their date searches.

When Denzil dials our friend James' number, the machine picks up. "Hey James, how's it going? Just calling to say you can't bring a date to the wedding. Got a problem with that, give me a call." He hangs up and I stare at him in shock.

"That was terrible, that was so rude, I'm embarrassed."

Denzil laughs and hands me the phone. "You try."

When I dial Alice's number, her machine picks up and I start to speak. "Err hi Alice, just calling to tell you that, well I don't mean to be a jerk about this, but the invitation to the wedding, well err, if you were planning to bring a date, I'm not sure how to say this, but don't. We have a limited number of people we can invite, and we don't really have enough room for people to bring guests. I'm sure you'll understand and I hope you're not offended. Thanks, bye."

By the end of the phone call I feel like an idiot. Of course people want to bring dates, it's a wedding. Going to a wedding alone can feel like a suicide mission. Though I also know that going with someone you're dating but aren't in love with can feel even worse. In the past when I went to weddings, if I wasn't in love with my date, listening to someone else's wedding vows inevitably underscored the reasons why. If I was in love but could tell the relationship wasn't headed toward marriage, my sadness was brought to the surface and made glaringly visible.

I remember a beautiful wedding on the beach in Malibu followed by a reception at a swank waterfront restaurant. Four couples were seated at the table, all friends and all desperately unhappy. The room seemed to be caught in a wave, the huge ocean swell of the bride and groom's happiness. The scale of their commitment, the glow of their smiles, created a standard from which the rest of us all very obviously fell short. Their celebration tucked dynamite in the cracks of the rest of our foundations, and within a month all four couples had broken up.

Still, I wish we'd thought about all this before and figured guests into the equation. I understand our friends' motivations, but after all the careful scaling down of our guest list it's growing like the blob.

Next I call Max. He picks up the phone and I start

into my practiced monologue, but having a person on the other end of the phone is making it much harder.

"Really?" Max asks disappointed. "I can't bring a date?"

"Sorry, it's just that we don't have enough room and we didn't really plan for it."

"Well, that's a problem," Max says "because I've already invited Jennifer and to un-invite her would be rude." I listen quietly. I'm dying to tell him that contrary to popular belief, you can put a price on friendship. Then I want to tell him that that price is $150. That's what we figure it's costing us per guest for food, alcohol, room rental, etc. I want to list all the people we actually know and like who we aren't inviting to the wedding. As I hem and haw, Denzil makes a slicing motion across his throat with his finger.

"Okay," I say half-heartedly, "One more guest won't kill us."

"Great, thanks, I'm sure you'll really like her."

# THE REGISTRY

It's nine o'clock on a Sunday morning in August and Cara is up and showered. This is very rare.

"What are you up to today?" I ask.

"I'm going to Golden Gate Park."

"Oh really," I say with a roller-coaster inflection, "with whom?"

"With Adam," Cara says casually while rummaging through the refrigerator.

"How old is this?" she asks, holding out a tub of yogurt.

"Too old." Denzil grabs the yogurt and tosses it into the trash. "How about some eggs?"

"Okay."

"Adam who?" I ask.

"Ignore her," Denzil says to Cara.

"Adam from my school."

"The kid with that amazing smile, right?" I ask.

"Right." Cara's face does something that looks a lot like blushing.

"I saw him smiling at you the other day when I dropped you off at school," I say. "Practically blinded me."

"How old is he?" I can't help but ask.

Denzil cracks several eggs into a metal bowl and makes a dramatic show of beating them, noisily clanking the fork against the metal bowl.

"Seventeen."

"How old are you?" Denzil asks.

"Fifteen."

"Just checking. Don't forget that."

"Don't worry," Cara says, "he's a Buddhist and a vegetarian."

"He's still a boy," Denzil says.


After breakfast Denzil and I go downstairs to clean our garage. The back half of the garage is piled with boxes and junk we couldn't find places for in the house when Cara and I moved in, and things of Denzil's that got squeezed out in the process.

"Look at all this crap," Denzil barks.

"Some of these things are treasures," I defend.

"And some of them are crap." He holds up a lamp base with a ballerina, as if to illustrate his point.

As far as I'm concerned, the lamp is too beautiful for words. I have two of them, a male dancer and a female dancer. When I found the lamps on the street two years ago, I couldn't believe someone was getting rid of them. I've yet to find the perfect place in the house to showcase their beauty, but I certainly haven't had the heart to pass them along.

"My mom asked again where we're registered," Denzil says.

This is the third time she's asked.

"Where are you registered?" is the first question we are asked when either of us speak to anyone from Denzil's family. Denzil's mom has three sisters but being with them all in one room they seem to multiply, creating a giggling, chattering, arguing force like a human tornado. Christmas, birthdays, marriages are all celebrated with gusto. After dinner and presents the karaoke machine is turned on, and for the rest of the party Denzil's mom and aunts snatch the microphone out of each other's hands and croon off-key renditions of half-forgotten Gershwin tunes, Supremes songs and Christmas carols.

I'm not used to this. I come from a family where it's practically ritual to forget each other's birthdays. We sometimes go years without exchanging gifts and at this point no one seems to care too much.

The whole registering thing has always rubbed me the wrong way. Maybe I'm lazy, but I can't imagine devoting several afternoons to faux shopping expeditions in which Denzil and I haggle over china patterns and flatware designs. Maybe I'm haunted by my own memories of looking through bridal registries and finding nothing I could afford to buy. Maybe I'm just don't like being told what gift I am supposed to give. Maybe I don't want our friends and family spending money on things we don't need.

"I don't want to register," I say.

"You're just being a rebel," Denzil accuses.

"I can't help it, it just feels creepy and greedy. I understand the concept of a wedding registry, and it makes perfect sense for a young couple setting up house for the first time. If people are going to buy you gifts anyway, they may as well give you things you want or need. But we aren't the young couple, and together we have more stuff than we know what to do with." I hold up a pair of roller blades and a wire CD rack, ready examples of our condition and my point.

"We still need a new toaster," Denzil says.

"That's true, we do need a toaster. But you probably don't need these," I say, holding up a pair of leather motorcycle gloves with frayed fingertips.

"I don't know what happened to those," Denzil says and tosses them in the trash.

"Do you know what happens when you aren't registered?" he asks, pulling something down from the back of a shelf. When he turns back he's holding a porcelain teddy bear cookie jar. "This is what happens."

"I wondered where that came from. Can I see it for a minute?" I take the cookie jar from Denzil and walk over to the trashcan. "You don't mind, do you?"

"No, I'm not sure why I kept it this long."

I drop the cookie jar and it makes a fantastic shattering sound: porcelain, metal, divorce and stupid jealousy dissolving into dusty shards. Admittedly, I know only one side of the story, but I can't imagine anything that would undo the protective rage that fills me when Denzil talks about finding his first wife in bed with someone else four months after their wedding.

But as Denzil looks into the trashcan I see something come over him, some thought or feeling that's not for me to understand. In a wave of compassion I realize that no matter how uncomfortable Denzil's past makes me, it's his and he deserves to hang on to as much of it as he wants, for as long as he wants. I have my own memories, lots of them. I drag sacks and sacks of them around with me wherever I go, dusting off this or that story to suit the occasion. I'm guessing, even hoping, that Denzil has a few good memories of his ex-wife to take some of the sting out of the bad ones.

"I'm sorry," I say. "That was crappy of me. That goofy bear might have meant something to you."

"Nothing good."

"You're not getting rid of these," Cara calls from the front of the garage where a big box of her ancient stuffed animals sits.

"We're just organizing," I assure her. "We won't get rid of anything important."

Denzil sorts through his camping equipment. I stack my easel and three large unfinished paintings against one wall of the garage. My box of oil paints is safely tucked away on a high shelf. I used to paint in my kitchen, in the old days when I didn't have oak tables and Oriental rugs to get in the way. Sometimes I miss the ease of not having nice things.

Cara pulls her furry creatures from the box and sets them up in a six-foot ring around her. She points at them one by one. "Betsy, Possum, Measles, Mumps, Rubella."

"What kind of names are those?" Denzil asks.

"When I was little I got a vaccine for measles, mumps and rubella. I thought they were the most beautiful names I'd ever heard. So I came home and named three of my favorite animals after them."

"Did your mom explain that those are diseases?" Denzil asks.

"I didn't want to spoil it for her."

Cara continued quizzing herself on animal names. "Scruffy, Bunny, Sam, Husband Bear..."

"Husband Bear?" Denzil repeats.

"I married him when I was three," Cara says, hugging the lopsided teddy bear. "We had a ceremony on the porch of our old house."

"Cool. I wish I'd been there."

Denzil grabs one end of the blue tarp and flips the other end at me. I pick up the two corners and walk toward him. "The only way to avoid getting gifts you don't want," Denzil says, "is to get no gifts at all."

"I'm okay with no gifts."

"If people really want to give us something, they can make a donation to charity," Denzil suggests.

"That's a good idea."

"Yeah, it makes us sound nice, but really we just don't want a bunch of junk we'll have to pretend to like and can't get rid of because the person who gave it to us might drop by."

Cara tosses her animals back into the box, reciting their names as she flings them from ten feet away. When a tall figure appears at the entrance to the garage, Cara quickly wings her last stuffed animal into the box and practically leaps toward him.

"This must be Adam," I say and walk toward them with my hand extended. "I'm Cara's mom and this is Denzil, Cara's stepdad-to-be."

Adam shakes my hand and says hello to both of us. He's thin and lanky, towering a full twelve inches over Cara's five-foot-two frame. He has straight brown hair, hazel eyes and a huge smile he can't seem to suppress. He is polite and, as far as I can tell, pretty much the teen dream date. His hand keeps wandering over to Cara's hand, and catching himself he draws it back to his side. Clearly he adores her. I find this so endearing I can barely suppress a giggle. I always thought this moment, no matter when it came, would feel like watching Cara climb on the back of a Harley and roll off into the distance, but seeing someone falling in love with her is wonderfully fulfilling. I silently congratulate myself on having raised someone so lovable, and with sense enough to date a sweet kid. Of all the things that freak me out about sending my child into the world, I'm relieved to find out, having a boyfriend isn't one of them.

Denzil and I send a postcard to everyone on our guest list saying:

*On the subject of gifts, we love burlwood clocks and brass-plated fondue dishes as much as the next happy couple, but aside from needing a toaster we have more than enough possessions to run a household. In lieu of gifts we would like to suggest you celebrate our marriage in one of the following ways.*

*A. Donate money to your favorite charity*

*B. Dance naked in a rainstorm*

*C. Call your mother once in a while, it won't kill you*

# THE CAKE

The cake is such a classic wedding icon, standing tall and white with the plastic bride and groom presiding over the reception hall. The cake's as important as the ring, the vows, the love that gets two people there in the first place. Cheesecake, beefcake, cupcake, fruitcake, all those sticky-sweet double entendres trapped in one four-letter word.

I don't really even like cake. In fact, I don't like cake at all. If given a piece I'll usually excavate the icing from the middle, and off the top and sides, and then pass the rest of it to Denzil. But still I imagine shopping for a wedding cake to be one of the easier, more pleasant tasks involved with planning a wedding.

The first sign of disappointment sneaks in when we park in front of the cinderblock bakery that's located behind a car dealership and marked with a hand-scrawled sign taped to the window. This bakery is one of the two City Club-approved bakeries. If we choose an approved supplier, the $2.50-per-slice cake-cutting fee the City Club charges will be waived.

The bakery has all the charm of a Depression-era steel mill. Mary, the baker, who's about as charmless as the bakery, seats us at a card table draped in a sticky plastic tablecloth. She hands us each a plastic fork and sets down a paper plate loaded with two-inch squares of various unfrosted cake samples.

It's in our best interest to like the cake. But I hate the cake. I hate the cake before I even taste it. After the first mouthful, I hate it even more. The cake tastes like it's been sitting on a shelf since the last royal wedding. I'm hard-pressed to find one I like better than the rest. Spice cake, chocolate cake, white cake, pound cake, yellow cake. The taste differences are minute; they all have the texture of a stale bread.

"This one isn't bad," Denzil says, aiming a forkful of khaki-colored cake at my mouth.

"Mmmmmm," I say, nodding politely for Mary's benefit, mostly because Mary scares me.

As we work on mouthfuls of dry cake, we flip through a photo album of cakes from weddings past. Between bites and vinyl sleeves of poorly lit photos of unspectacular wedding cakes, I remember that the best part of my previous wedding was the cake. I'm happy that I've finally remembered something nice about that day, but right now the memory isn't helpful. It was from a small Dutch bakery. It was rich chocolate with raspberry filling and frosted with thick curls of shaved white chocolate. Each of the three tiers was decorated with beautiful pink tea roses.

"How much are your cakes?" I ask.

Mary rolls her eyes. "I don't even turn on my oven for less than $850."

"How hard can it be to bake a cake?" I want to ask,

but I get the feeling she may reach over the card table and strangle me if I do. Something about this woman makes me think she may have learned cake decorating in jail. Maybe it's her three-packs-a-day voice, or maybe the scar that reaches from eye to jawbone, which doesn't strike me as the result of a cake-decorating accident. We tell Mary we're going to think about things for a few days before ordering the cake.

As we drive away from the bakery I am in a foul mood. The memory of my other, beautiful wedding cake has thrown me. I always find it easier to live with the bad memories of my past than the good, as they so effortlessly underscore the reasons I'm not there anymore. The bad memories justify the disappointment of divorce; it's the good memories that trip me up. I funnel this flash of angst into an impassioned rant. "There is no way in hell I'm going to spend $850 on a cake. That is ridiculous. I'll serve a mound of Hostess cupcakes before I'll pay that woman $850 to dust off one of her stale cakes and toss a few flowers on it."

"How hard can it be to bake a cake?" I say to Denzil.

"How hard can it be?" he repeats. "It's just a cake."

"You're a good cook, I bet you could do it," I say. My cooking style doesn't really suit precision endeavors such as baking.

"The timing could be a little tricky, but I bet we could work it out."

"Even if we spend a hundred dollars on materials, and pay the cake-cutting fee, we still come out ahead," I say.

In the thirty minutes it takes us to get home, we have agreed to take on the project of baking our own wedding cake.

"Are you sure this is a good idea?" I ask.

"No worse than paying a full week's salary for stale cake," Denzil says.

Denzil quickly embraces the idea of baking the cake. He makes it his mission. He immerses himself in cake. He buys baking magazines and cake books. He orders cake for dessert at restaurants.

When I tell Luchi our plan to make our own cake, she insists on helping. Luchi is the most generous person I know, but also the most overbooked. I can see a fumbling "I Love Lucy"-style escapade in the making, but I'm really happy she's going to be involved. The plan is that Denzil will buy all the ingredients and get everything ready, then the day before the wedding Luchi will come to our house and bake and frost the cake.

Over the next three weeks, Denzil bakes no fewer than seven cakes. Whole days are devoted to the cake project. He makes chocolate cake with buttercream frosting, white cake with whipped cream frosting, almond vanilla cake with lemon curd filling, yellow cake with white chocolate frosting. There are no shortcuts, he makes everything from scratch. Everything in the kitchen is coated in a fine layer of white powder.

Denzil's reaction to stress is to make the simplest issues into complex problems. At the hands of an anxious Denzil, choosing the filling for a layer cake can turn into an equation on par with finding pi. I've never seen someone whip themselves into such a frenzy over baking. It's scaring me a little but I find it endearing.

Cara and I are the official cake tasters and we are cross-examined after each tasting. "Can you taste the vanilla?" Denzil asks. "Does it melt or crumble in your mouth?" "Would you say it has a delicate or a heavy flavor?" "I baked this one at 325 and the last one at 350, can you tell the difference?"

We have roundtable discussions weighing the virtues and categorizing the faults of each and every cake. Taste, texture, presentation, frostability, sliceability.

This sort of picayune analysis comes easily for Denzil. This sort of picayune analysis makes me and Cara crazy. Denzil is showing tremendous perseverance. Luchi is showing tremendous patience. I'm wishing we spent the $850.

# SAMBA ANXIETISTA

It's 7:30 on a Tuesday night in September and I'm standing on the front steps waiting for Denzil. He finally gallops down the stairs and out the front door. "Jesus Christ," I say with clenched jaw. "Can't you ever just put on your coat and leave the house?"

Denzil gives me an angry look over his shoulder as he locks the door. With the wedding less than a month away, little things seem big and the big things seem bigger. I see myself in twenty years still waiting for Denzil to remember all the things he's forgotten inside, up and down the stairs three times before he gets it together to actually leave the house. I wonder how I'll find the patience to deal with it. I wonder if we should even get married if I'm going to spend half of our married life standing on the porch while Denzil looks for his hat. I fear I'm much better suited to being a mother than a wife. Marriage is a cooperative effort, filled with compromises and negotiation. Negotiation isn't necessary when someone is small enough to be picked up and carried out of the house.

"Damn, I forgot my water. Oops," I say sheepishly and grab the key from Denzil's hand. "I'll be right back."

"Did you remember to call the City Club today?" I ask as I climb into the car.

"No, never got a chance."

"You were going to call them three days ago."

"I've been busy."

"Well, if you don't want to call them, then just say you don't want to call them and I'll call them."

"I said I'd call them."

"When?"

Denzil guns it around a corner. "Is this how it's going to be? You nagging me about all the stupid little things you think I should do? We're not even married and you already sound like a *wife*."

My hand clenches the armrest and squeezes. I hate the word "wife." It feels weighty, loaded with expectations; it recalls housecoats and baked goods. Wives get electric brooms for their birthdays. They complain about their husbands and embark on retaliatory shopping expeditions. The title has an uptight respectability that makes me uncomfortable. Wives are women who don't like me, women who glare at me at dinner parties if they think I've talked to their husbands for too long. A wife is someone to avoid–the enemy of a good time–and all I can think is that I don't want to be one. I am reminded that the twelve years it's taken me to even consider getting married again have been no accident.

"Forget it," I say.

"Forget what?"

"All of it."

"All of what?"

"Everything, the wedding, the phone calls, the fall-colored floral arrangements, the $250 dollar shoes. Just forget all of it. I don't want to be a wife."

"Do you mean that?" Denzil asks.

"Probably not," I answer.

We are silent until we arrive at the dance studio. We can hear the music when we get out of the car on Mission Street. Denzil pulls his drum from the back of the car as I scramble up the stairs. I toss my bag on the bench and find a place on the floor, sit down and split my legs out to the side as far as I can. The stretch feels good in a painful, tugging sort of way, but mostly I am marking my territory, claiming my five square feet of real estate so that I'll be able to do the warm-up without knocking my foot into someone else's shoulder.

Denzil joins the other drummers with his conga, and the music becomes louder, the energy steps up a notch. I remember that I forgot to call the caterer to change the pizzettas to smoked salmon on toast points. I do endless sit-ups and lose myself in the music, in the movement. The music pushes out the thoughts. I stop thinking about my wedding shoes and Denzil's tux, I stop thinking about the word "wife." I stop worrying about our swelling guest list, about chicken or fish or what sort of goddamn wedding cake to serve.

We are a rag-tag collection of dancers of all levels, in all shapes and sizes, mostly women but with the occasional man. We wear Lycra and colorful sarongs, sweatpants and gym shorts, sexy halter tops and tight black pants. We jump, leap, turn, plant our feet and shake our hips one way, our shoulders another. Our arms reach and scoop, then pull up overhead as we step behind then jump sideways. This crazy Saint Vitus dance may have been what Arthur Murray would have come up with if he'd visited Brazilian Carnival, come home and started experimenting with hallucinogenic drugs.

Rhonda, our instructor, looks like a roller derby queen. A fringed scarf hugs her hips, glints of light flash off her beaded top. To watch her dance is an inspiration. Her talent lights up the room with the magic that comes from someone who has recognized her gifts, and done the work to develop them into an art.

In any given class we may learn three separate dances in different Brazilian styles. None any easier, less strenuous, or slower than the others. Samba, which is a combination of tiny complicated steps executed at lightning speed. Orisha dances, which are derived from African religious ceremonies, and whose movements are bold, fast and narrative. And Samba Reggae, which is a combination of fast movements done to an impossibly bouncy tempo.

After the grueling warm-up we organize ourselves into five lines of about a dozen people each. Rhonda introduces the choreography, a dance for Xangao the Orisha warrior god, at half-tempo, then just as we begin to catch on she throws herself into rhythmic overdrive. She is beautiful, a ball of fire with perfect rhythm. Her shoulders quiver, her hips move fast, her feet are more off the ground than on as she glides and spins across the floor. She makes it look easy. Ecstatic yelps burst out of the crowd. We try to follow the choreography but our movements blend together. We each have different interpretations of what we just saw her do. By the time the entire class has made it across the floor, the dance has mutated into something barely recognizable. We twirl and stomp on snakes, we throw lightening bolts and fend off imaginary enemies with imaginary axes.

I've been studying Brazilian dance three days a week for just over three years. With most disciplines, this level

of practice and commitment would render me compe-
tent. With that much practice it wouldn't be unreasonable to think that I might even be good. Brazilian dance
doesn't work like that. Good is a long-term goal, more of
a holy grail than an actual target. I'm not saying I
haven't made progress. I have slowly moved through the
ranks of bad, terrible, and dangerously unskilled, to
someone who looks like she may be trying to dance.

When I look across the room at Denzil, he's lost in
the music. He's been drumming for this class since
shortly after we started dating. Denzil's played drums
since he was a kid, and he took to the Brazilian rhythms
easily. The drummers are crowded into one corner.
Denzil has his shirt off and his chest muscles flex with
each slap of the drum. Denzil's mother is Italian and his
father is Anglo-Indian. His skin is the color of milky tea
and his frame is thin and strong. His features are delicate
and chiseled, an angular jaw, thin equine nose, and large
brown eyes framed by wire-rimmed glasses. Beneath his
eyes are dark circles that give away his Indian heritage.
From where I stand I can see a lattice of muscles rum-
bling across his bare back as he drums and I am reminded
of how sexy I think he is. A "wife" isn't supposed to
think these sorts of things, which makes the prospect of
being one more inviting.

I remember how long I looked for Denzil. How many
men I dated hoping to find him. I remember the way I
trust him, and the way he treats Cara. I think about our
home and the curtains I'm making for the front room.
Then I think that rewriting the wife handbook should-
n't be that difficult. Here, in this class, surrounded by
creativity and energy, music and movement, and people
striving to be better than they are, I feel confident I can
create a version of wife that I would like to be.

I let the rhythm flood me, I pray for the music to drown out the thought, to drown out the voice that tells me I can't dance, that says I'm too old, too embarrassed to ever be good. My feet become wings, my shoulders shimmy, my hips slide back and forth, my feet skip and fly. From the corners of my eyes I see the two dancers next to me, and we move in perfect synchronicity. Either I'm doing it right, or we're all doing it wrong. I catch a glimpse of myself in the mirror, and I look like a dancer.

There is magic happening on the dance floor. One hundred feet are dancing in unison, fifty dancers laced together by the rhythm of the music. The whole room riding the same breath. I am stunned, seduced by the beauty of this foreign ritual I have claimed as my own.

On the way home my clothes are damp and I am riding the calm of exhaustion. Denzil is pounding out a left-over rhythm on the steering wheel.

"I changed my mind."

"About what?"

"I think I'd like to marry you, if that's okay."

"Okay," Denzil says. He looks at me and smiles.

"What would you think about hiring the band from class to play our wedding?" I ask.

"I think that's a great idea."

"Good, I'll arrange it," I add as a peace offering.

"We can have cake when we get home," Denzil says, and I know it's his version of a peace offering.

Denzil has spent all afternoon baking another cake. This one is yellow with buttercream frosting, which for some reason has turned out battleship gray. I smile. I'm so sick of cake I could die.

# THE TUXEDO

The next morning I ask Denzil if he's thought any more about what he's going to wear to the wedding. I know the answer, but something, that lurking part of me that is always ready to reach for the gas can when I see the flicker of something that looks inflammable, prods me to ask anyway.

"I don't see any reason not to wear my tuxedo."

"How old is that tuxedo?" I ask.

"I don't know, five or six years."

"Around the time of your first wedding, perhaps?"

"Yeah. So?"

"So?" I shout as I leap up from the breakfast table. "How can you even consider getting married in the same clothes you wore to your first wedding? This is a special occasion. It's a sacred occasion. You are entering a new life, you need new clothes."

"I'd wear a different shirt."

"Maybe I should just dust off my old wedding dress. I'm sure I have it around here somewhere."

"Weren't you six months pregnant last time you got married?"

"So?" I say, grabbing a pillow off the chair and shoving it under my bathrobe. I waddle across the room. "Why buy a new wedding dress when I already have a perfectly fine one hanging in my closet. Why waste the money. Hell, I only wore it once. A wedding dress should last a lifetime, no matter how many weddings a girl has."

I actually don't know why I kept it. The day I plopped down $75 for the dress that looked like a box of lace handkerchiefs stitched together with a crochet needle, I knew I'd never wear it again. Now Cara will have two to choose from, depending on the circumstances, though I really hope she doesn't need the maternity gown.

"Tuxedos are different," Denzil tries to explain.

"Does anything about this idea strike you as being in poor taste? It doesn't seem like bad luck to wear the same clothes to your second wedding as you did to your first?" I take the pillow out of my robe and toss it at him. "How can you be such a moron?"

"I doubt my first marriage didn't work out because of the suit I got married in."

"Yeah, well," I stammer, walking out of the room, "it could have everything to do with why your second doesn't."

"What did you say?"

"I said we can talk about it some other time!" I shout from the hallway.

I stomp into the living room and think that a woman would never recycle her wedding clothes. I could do an exit poll outside a convent and all the nuns would understand the faulty logic at play here. Women are from Venus and men are missing part of their frontal lobe.

I shuffle through my stacks of CDs looking for the

perfect song to match my mood. Music to express how stupid I think men are, a song to shout Denzil down without having to raise my voice. Something to burn off the jealousy, because of course all I can think about is Denzil getting undressed on his wedding night, his first wedding night.

I slip an Aimee Mann CD into the stereo and turn it up too loud for a Sunday morning. I plop down on the futon in the living room and stare out at the line of blackbirds sitting at the edge of the rooftop across the street. What am I doing, I think, what the hell am I doing? Is this really where I want to be? Of all the places I have been, am I the happiest here? Do I have pre-wedding jitters, cold feet, or are my concerns more serious than that?

The blackbirds suddenly abandon their perch. In a flurry of cries and feathers, they swoop from sight, and it looks so easy, so inviting. Just fly away. Suddenly I am flooded with doubt. It's not that Denzil wants to wear the same clothing to his second wedding as he did to his first. It's bigger than that, and smaller, much smaller. It's about my life at its most elemental. It's about not having to answer questions about what I am doing and when I'll be done doing it, or why I left my socks on the chair in the entry hall, or why I only drank half my tea. It's about climbing into bed at night, turning off the light and watching the moon outside the bedroom window as the day unravels in my mind and not having the spell broken by someone slipping into bed beside me. It's about owning the room, owning the time and the quiet. It's about saying goodbye to the deep calm of aloneness.

I feel panicked at the thought of giving up these simple freedoms and I can't help but think about the boyfriends I've had who I was content just to look at.

Looking at them, admiring their beauty and reveling in their adoration was the beginning and the end. I didn't need to know what they were thinking. I didn't need to wend my way through their seaweed thoughts. I didn't need to understand their philosophical beliefs. Likewise, there was no need for them to know my insurance payment was two weeks late and what time my daughter needed to get to her orthodontist appointment. These relationships took place in the margins. In the spaces between dropping Cara off at school and picking her up in the afternoon, on the weekends when she visited her father and the midnight pixie hours. The lines of intimacy, real intimacy—messy, raw and terribly inconvenient—were never crossed.

Denzil comes into the living room and sits down beside me. He leans his head on my shoulder. "I just got off the phone with my sister," he says. "She agrees with you."

"About what?" I mumble.

"That I'm a moron, and about the tux. She agrees it would be in bad taste to wear it. Sorry, I'll wear something else."

"That would be nice," I say, and continue to stare out the window.

"Doesn't it ever scare you?" I ask.

"What?"

"All of it, getting married, the idea of spending the rest of your life with me. Sharing your bed, and the kitchen and the coat closet. Having to answer to someone about where you've been and what you've been doing."

"Apparently not as much as it scares you," Denzil replies. We sit quietly for a moment and listen to the music. One by one the blackbirds come back to their rooftop perch.

Denzil lays his head in my lap. "I've been waiting for this my whole life. I've spent enough time alone and now that I've got a family, I like it."

This melts me. I scan through the list of grievances and fears that seemed so overwhelming twenty minutes ago and I'm not sure what I was so upset about. It's so much easier to forgive someone who can admit they're wrong.

# THE MUSIC

For months I've been obsessed with what music we're going to have at the wedding. Scribbling lists, sifting through my CD collection, playing song after song after song. We need music for when the guests arrive, for the processional, the recessional, cocktails, dinner and the first dance. I dream of the music, the wrong music. I dreamt there was no sound system and I was begging our minister to go home and get his speakers. In one dream I heard the theme music from the film *Merry Christmas, Mr. Lawrence*. The entire piano composition played through my dream and I kept thinking it would be perfect for the processional, but then I decided it might be inappropriate because it came from a film about a Japanese P.O.W. camp.

I scour my music collection for potential wedding songs. I read title after title and hear the songs in my head, word for word, note for note. Like surprise wafts of perfume they send me back to glimmers of my past, friends, lovers, road trips. Whole eras live on these shelves. Everything reminds me of something, but nothing I want to incorporate into my wedding.

I flip through the racks of used CDs at the music store. The rhythmic clicking fills me with anticipation. I feel at home here. Here where I am surrounded by possibility, where at any moment I could flip from one CD to the next, and happen upon that elusive Nick Drake or Go-Betweens CD. The one I've been hunting for for the past three years, the one that's been out of print for the last five. I keep looking, keep clicking, keep searching, knowing my efforts may be rewarded by finding a reissue of Robert Palmer's first album, *Sneakin' Sally Through the Alley*, a CD I've been trying to find for the past ten years.

"Who cares about the music?" Denzil asked yesterday. "Of all the things to worry about, music is the last on my list." I can't believe what I'm hearing. My ears are offended, I am offended, my music collection is offended. The soundtrack to my life has, at times, been more interesting than my life itself. I've been known to fall in love on the strength of a good compilation tape, and fall out of love because someone used the words "I like" and "Billy Joel" in the same paragraph. I am a snob, an unabashed music snob. The focus of my snobbery isn't limited to people who listen to what I deem to be bad music; I freely extend my disdain to people who don't care about music at all. I think there is something wrong with people who don't need music. I think people who would rather sit in silence than be troubled to turn on the radio or change the CD are lazy at best, and at worst, soulless and boring. I fear that the man I am about to commit to spending my life with may be one of these people and I fear that love has made the edges of reality all fuzzy.

For me, buying CDs is both celebration and vice. The record store is the place I come when I am upset, depressed, bored, or happy. Sad guys with guitars have been my musical accompaniment throughout most of my life. They've sung me out of one heartbreak and into another since I was seven years old and had my first crush. I am in strange company at this oasis—my comrades in musical obsession are generally men in their mid-30s, usually paunchy with bald spots. Men who can rattle off album release dates and band lineups with the savant dexterity of a Yankees' fan reciting baseball scores. Men who have the complete works of Tom Waits, including the 1999 Japanese import. All of us, these men and I, are ready to spend our grocery money on 30 minutes of beauty, on a dose of magic to pull us through love and hate and heartbreak. Rhythmic testimonials to sentiments we may or may not have felt but in that moment can claim as our own. Each song a three-minute journey into a stranger's heart. Fascinated, all of us, by the power to create beauty, to put words to music and melt hearts. We are the ones for whom music is made, we are the other half of the equation. Nothing is more important than a fan.

But Denzil is a musician, and a good one. He pounds out rhythms incessantly, on steering wheels, drumheads, on his lap and my back. Other musicians want to play with him. I decide that playing music must lessen the innate need to consume it, and that Denzil's musical abilities afford him special dispensation. I choose to believe this, to bank on it because right now I am neck-deep in wedding plans and I have no room in my cluttered brain for any unpleasant realizations.

The soft click of plastic jewel cases knocking against each other is mesmerizing. I flip through the Brazilian section, I try to decipher the Portuguese writing on the backs of CD cases. I look for familiar names or words. I pick up a promising-looking compilation album. I slip the open end of the CD holder around my arm like a bracelet and head for the reggae section. I find the Jimmy Cliff version of "I Can See Clearly Now" that I heard on the radio late last night. It's a cornball song, but it always makes me cry. Carole King's overplayed hit would be too pedestrian, but Jimmy Cliff's rendition is obscure enough to make it seem more like an original idea for a first dance song.

I move along to the rock section. As I look through the titles memories wash over me. The Beatles: nine years old, lying in bed listening to the radio and diligently trying to learn all the lyrics to "Norwegian Wood." Neil Young: seventh grade, making out with Randy Brown in the tack trailer at his parents' horse ranch. David Bowie's *Diamond Dogs*: given to me by Brian Cunningham for my fourteenth birthday. Blue Oyster Cult: fifteen, my first concert, a velvet-lined Sucrets box filled with joints and four-inch blue platform shoes I shop-lifted with Nina Taylor. The Jam: Nineteen, wearing short skirts from the thrift store and wanting to be British. Elvis Costello's *Blood and Chocolate* album, the breakup of my marriage. Nick Cave: Drum cigarettes and whiskey on the deck after my daughter had fallen asleep.

I move from aisle to aisle, flipping through the racks with precision and myopic focus. Searching, searching, working my way through the alphabet of the used CDs, my eyes rapidly shifting from one title to the next. Lou Reed plays on the overhead stereo. The song ends and nothing replaces it. We all look up, startled, like children woken from a nap too soon. The room fills with an orchestra of soft click-clicking, plastic on plastic like Southern cicadas, like court stenographers, like a secretarial pool working on a sea of manual typewriters. The clerk puts on Lucinda Williams and we all go back to our business.

A bored girlfriend clutches her new Sade album and stands at the end of the aisle waiting for her boyfriend. He glances over to her as he's flipping through the "W" section of used jazz, his arm loaded with CDs. She gives him the look. The look that gives away her ignorance, the look that says his magic is her inconvenience. She is oblivious to the fact that he is hunting, hunting for music that may unwittingly become the soundtrack for a part of her life. Music that may in time trigger memories, sweet memories, bitter memories. Music to paint her world.

When they get home he'll sit her down and say, "You have to hear this song." He'll talk in an animated tone, with excitement, real excitement, the way he used to talk about her to his friends, back when they first met, back when she found his music collection impressive. Back when they would stay up all night, with him playing her song after song, each one telling her something he couldn't.

But she'll just want to hear her Sade album. She's been defending her musical taste for years with weak arguments like "It's good background music, I don't really have to listen to it," and "It's so pretty."

He doesn't want music to be easy. He wants music to fill up the room, not to fill in the leftover spaces. Music is a passion, a dance partner, a friend, a lover. Songs tell him stories, they take him places, they are the elixir, the red hot poker, a place to feel better, a place to feel worse. He invites her to travel with him, but if she can't, he'll fly away on his own. Fly away with Charlie Parker, climb into bed with Nina Simone, have a drink with Billie Holiday.

I leave the store with a heavy bag. I walk home quickly, carried by excitement and anticipation. When I get home I fumble with the plastic wrapper on the Jimmy Cliff CD. I put the disc in the stereo and call Denzil into the living room. Goon-ka-shaka-shaka. Goon-ka-shaka-shaka. Jimmy Cliff's voice fills the room. I pull Denzil's arms around my waist and make him dance with me.

"What do you think?" I ask.

"About what?"

"About 'I Can See Clearly Now' for a first dance song?"

Denzil stops moving and listens hard. "Seems okay," he says, "I mean it's a little cheesy, but I guess it could work."

I love the song. Hearing it has made my eyes well up. I rub them miming a terrible itch, trying to hide the fact that I really am a hopeless romantic. When the song ends Denzil leaves the room. I lie on the floor and listen to the next song. I close my eyes and let the music surround me and remember the first time I saw Denzil dance, really dance. We were at a wedding in Minneapolis last spring. It was nearing the end of the night and a band called Trailer Trash was ripping through versions of everything from Glenn Campbell's "Wichita Lineman," to Hank Williams' "Lonesome Road." I pulled Denzil onto the dance floor during a sweet, rolling tune. He put his hands on my hips and we danced in slow gliding motions. The song ended and the band quickly segued into a loud fast version of Johnny Burnette's "Rockabilly Boogie." Denzil launched himself across the floor like a clown shot out of a cannon. He landed and spun, leapt up, bounced then turned. His arms swung from side to side, counterbalancing the manic motion of his legs. He jerked his head first one way then the other while catapulting himself across the dance floor over and over again.

Not sure how to react, I kept dancing, spun, kicked my feet, pretended not to notice Denzil's crazy dance. One by one, the other dancers cleared the floor. A crowd started to gather. Grandmothers pulled themselves up from floral couches and came to the edge of the dance floor and stared. Young women clutched their sides and bellowed with laughter.

I tried to move a little faster, to bounce a little more, but with Denzil ejecting himself from one corner to the next, I wasn't sure how to keep pace and still have all my teeth at the end of the dance. I backed to the edge of the dance floor and joined the crowd where I was greeted with raised eyebrows and approving or disapproving winks. Their looks implied culpability, guilt by association. I shrugged my shoulders, I had no explanation, I had never seen anything like this before either.

I'm the one who spends two hours, three days a week stretching and pulling and training my body. I'm supposed to be the dancer, but all I could do was stand clear and watch.

Denzil kept dancing. Movements I didn't know were possible, movements I didn't know he was capable of performing with such lithe ease he executed with an awesome childish abandon.

Denzil is given to this sort of unpredictable silliness. Moments when spontaneous creativity leaks out of his polished exterior. Denzil is trim and athletic without the least effort. He can go without food or sleep and exhibit none of the hunched-over whining I am prone to when tired or hungry. His mind is agile and well-trained, his clothes are never rumpled or stained and his bank account is always balanced. To see him fly around the dance floor like this is to see a crack in the façade, a crack out of which shines a beautiful, brilliant light. I watched him twist and fly and couldn't help but wonder what would have happened if he hadn't been raised by two accountants.

The bride's brother, a heavy-set biker, pulled his ol' lady onto the dance floor, wrapped his thick arms around her waist and proceeded to toss her around like a sack of flour. Others grabbed partners, or leapt onto the floor solo. The room became alive with whirling chaos.

My heart welled with pride at the infectious magic Denzil had inspired. I stepped onto the dance floor and joined the melee. Gray-haired men with loosened ties twirled their arms and skipped. Overweight women in square-cut dresses shook their backsides, heads slung back and forth, people bounced into one another, stepped on toes and no one seemed to mind. The bride and groom grabbed hands and spun in wide circles in the center of the dance floor, bumping into children who tumbled into bridesmaids.

It was beautiful. But remembering the display did leave me with the nagging question of what was going to happen at our wedding.

As I lie on the floor, I feel something warm beside me. Denzil slides his hand onto my belly and lays his head on my shoulder. We lie there, still and silent, until the CD is over.

# THE JOYS OF PARENTHOOD

It's a warm Friday afternoon in September and as I turn into the parking lot of Cara's school my muffler scrapes against the driveway, making a terrible noise. Cara's high school is small, fewer than a hundred kids. It's housed in the Greek Orthodox Church half a block from Valencia Gardens, the euphemistic name for some of the worst housing projects in San Francisco. Last Tuesday someone was shot on the corner one block away from the school and an impromptu shrine has developed with flowers and photographs and candles. The kids aren't bothered. I suspect they think it's sort of cool in a gruesome horror movie sort of way. They still believe they are invincible. I know they aren't. I know that very bad things happen. At fifteen I was running wild–stuffing my bed and sneaking out my window. Hiking three miles up and over a range of foothills to visit my boyfriend, who I'd been forbidden to see. Hitchhiking across town at midnight. Going to parties with people twice my age. I lie awake thinking about the things that could happen to Cara, cataloguing them, making emotional damage assessments and assigning imaginary recovery times.

This neighborhood is always a little creepy on Friday afternoons when the rumble of the weekend begins. Men in warm-up suits with do-rags tied on their heads lean against walls like graffiti. Skinny prostitutes of indeterminate gender approach your car if you stare for a few seconds too long. Sometimes it's easier for me to drive across town and pick Cara up than to worry about her getting home safely.

I've just come from an appointment with the florist where I've learned that flowers for the wedding—fleeting but beautiful and strangely important—will cost slightly less than half a semester's tuition at my daughter's school. But once again I've been swept away, caught in the wedding whirlwind whereby seemingly unimportant things take on unfounded significance. Where desire becomes a bulldozer, shoving aside logic and good sense and practicality.

I've been romanced by the florist's portfolio. Rich, glossy prints of bridal bouquets of roses and freesia with trailing ribbons of green and blue silk. Table arrangements in deep fall colors—reds, oranges, golds and greens—spilling over with pomegranates and persimmons and set in antique silver vases. I've committed to the whole lot and now I need only write a check for $3,500 and choose the ribbon color for the bridal party bouquets. I feel a little sick. I look out at the chipped paint on the buildings across the street and the 8-foot fence that surrounds the entire block, and I think $3,500 could make a big difference in this neighborhood.

After classes are dismissed, milling teenagers flood the courtyard. I stare at the sea of kids lugging overstuffed backpacks and as always I'm surprised by how difficult it is to pick my kid out of the lineup. From the slightest distance, all of the girls look the same; long hair pulled back into messy ponytails, Dickies pants worn low on their hips, and tight tank tops with colored bra straps peeking out. A clashing mixture of hippy earthiness and urban teenage funk.

Cara no longer cringes when I arrive to pick her up. The adventure and thrill of independence that came with taking the bus has mellowed into a world-weary dread of the long ride home. She climbs into the car.

"Mommy," she says. I know any sentence beginning with "Mommy" is going to involve some sort of effort on my part.

"Yes, darling," I answer with a sing-song flourish.

"Are you and Denzil going out tonight?"

"Why?" I ask.

"Because I want to have a slumber party at our house."

"Of course you do," I say. "And what are you going to do at this slumber party?"

"I don't know, maybe go down to Haight Street for a little while, watch movies, get a pizza, the normal stuff."

I can tell there is mischief afoot, I can feel it. Nothing she says gives away her intention, but I know it's there. I know it the same way my mom always knew when I had lied about where I was going to spend the night, or if I had gone to the beach instead of to school.

"Who are you going to invite?" I ask, knowing it doesn't really matter, all of them are just as good and just as bad as the others.

"Just Courtney and Rhian and Rose."

The usual suspects. I've known all these girls since they were four years old. Most of them are taller than I am now, and I've never really gotten used to the fact that

I am the adult.

"Sure," I say, "you can have your friends over." My stomach tells me this is a bad idea, but whatever they're cooking up I'd rather it take place at our house where I'll have the opportunity to intervene. I subscribe to the theory that I'd rather have the kids do what they're going to do under my roof, but I hate when I have to employ it.

"When will you guys be home?" Cara asks.

Denzil and I have plans to go out to dinner and then to a birthday party, but during the short drive home I have reshuffled our plans.

"Around ten," I say. "We're just going to dinner."

All through dinner I am anxious. I check my watch and squirm in my chair. I've told the girls they can go to Haight Street, but they need to be home by 10 o'clock. I pull the bundle of ribbons out of my purse in an attempt to distract myself.

"What color do you like best?" I ask, sliding the ribbons toward Denzil.

"All of them."

"That's not helpful."

At nine forty-five I call the house. There's no answer. My belly churns with intuition or panic or just plain sadness that my child is growing up.

When Denzil and I arrive home just after ten I'm already in a sweat.

"Stay in the car," I say as I leap out.

I unlock the front door and dash up the stairs, shouting hello to Cara and her friends. No one responds. I walk down the hall, past the living room, past Cara's room. The house is empty. I walk into the kitchen. The light on the answering machine blinks, so I push the button and let the message play. "Ahhhh, hey, this is the pizza guy, I'm at your front door. Hello, is anybody there?" As the message plays I turn and see two enormous beer bottles on the counter. Olde English 800 malt liquor, the same crap we used to drink. One bottle is empty, the other is gone except for a couple of inches. I run back downstairs and jump in the car.

"Drive," I order Denzil.

"What do you mean 'drive'?" Denzil says.

"Just drive, go down the hill, go down to Haight."

"Why?" Denzil asks.

"Because the girls are drunk."

"How do you know?"

"Because there are two 40-ouncer bottles on the kitchen counter, and they've been drinking that swill on an empty stomach."

"How do you know *that?*"

"There's a message on the answering machine from the pizza guy. He was trying to deliver the pizza but the girls didn't answer the door."

Denzil starts to look a little panicked. "I'm wearing clogs, I've got to change my shoes," he says.

"No you don't, you need to drive to Haight Street."

"It'll just take a second. I can't run in these shoes."

Denzil must have visions of chasing the kids down alleys, scrambling over chain-link fences, toppled garbage cans, barking Dobermans. But right now mother's intuition trumps Denzil's action-hero fantasy.

"Jesus Christ, Denzil, no one's asking you to run, can you please just drive to Haight Street."

"And what are we going to do, drive around looking for them?"

"Yeah."

Reluctantly, Denzil backs out of the driveway and heads down the hill. "How do you know they're there?"

"I just know."

"Turn left," I say when we reach Haight. We round the corner. One block down on the right-hand side, there is an ambulance. Beside the ambulance there are two cops and three of the four girls. I am not surprised.

Denzil pulls in behind the ambulance, the swirling lights bathing us in red. I leap out before the car comes to a full stop. Cara sees me and makes an attempt to run in the opposite direction. Rose and Rhian each catch an arm.

I hear a wailing sound coming from the ambulance and look through the window. Courtney is in the back. Her face is wet from sobbing, her hair hangs in a messy tangle, she looks frantic like an animal in a trap, but she is very much alive and this is all I care about.

I walk over to the girls, who are all in tears.

"What the hell is going on here?" I shout, not really expecting much of an answer.

I turn toward the policemen. I want to grab their legs and kiss their feet. "Thank you so much for keeping these kids out of trouble," I say, and immediately feel stupid. It's obvious they are in more trouble than any of them could have imagined. Four little private-school girls, weathering a failed attempt at big-kid partying. Not only are they in trouble, they are being humiliated by the constant parade of snickering tourists and Haight Street veterans, all witnessing their folly.

"Are you the mother of one of these girls?" one of the cop asks me.

I nod yes. "What happened?"

"Well, obviously the girls are drunk. Those three aren't so bad, but the one in the ambulance, she told us her name was," he looked down at his notes, "Monique Shelly, then she told us her name was Lori Frederick."

I had to laugh. Courtney is Chinese, one hundred percent Chinese. Her last name is Lee. Nothing about her looks like a Shelly or a Frederick. Monique and Lori are perfect blonde bunny girls Cara and her friends can't stand. I'm surprised she can be drunk as a sailor and still this resourceful.

"Her name is Courtney."

"Whoever she is, she's very drunk, and her foot needs attention."

"How bad is her foot?"

"She needs ten or twelve stitches, but we're more concerned about the amount of alcohol in her."

"Can you just release her to us and we'll get her to the hospital?" Denzil asks.

"She's already logged into our system."

"And the others?" I ask, looking at Cara, Rose and Rhian, huddled together like plane crash survivors.

"They were all pretty cooperative, and none of them seem as drunk as their friend."

Denzil and I load the kids into the car and follow the ambulance to the hospital. I am quietly determined to have these girls at ground zero of the aftermath. They are already terrified, but I want them to be even more terrified. This is an educational opportunity and if I can push away that aching feeling of wanting to protect them from the rest of the unpleasantries this night has in store for us, they'll have learned a good lesson.

"How drunk are you girls?" I ask as I lean over the back of my seat.

"Not as drunk as Courtney," Cara answers.

"No, not nearly as drunk," Rhian adds.

"Why did Courtney get so drunk?" I ask.

Cara tilts her head down and raises her eyebrows, giving me the *I can't believe how stupid you are* look.

"Because she drank more."

"We told her not to drink so much but she just kept drinking," Rhian said.

"What were you doing on the bus?"

"We went to meet some of Courtney's friends and we were going to be back by ten," Cara says, "but when we got up to Geary Street Courtney could hardly stand up."

"We didn't know what to do," Rhian said, "she wanted to lay down on the sidewalk but we made her keep walking."

"We waited forever for the bus. Some guys stopped and asked if we needed a ride, but we said no," Rose said.

"That was good," Denzil says in a parental tone.

"When the bus finally came we got on, and when we got to our stop Courtney was standing on the step by the door," Cara explained. "The doors opened right onto her foot. She started screaming and screaming. It took two men to get the door off her foot. She kept screaming and people started gathering around us, then the police came, then the ambulance."

I'm amazed at what a scene their attempt to have a little fun has caused. I listen to their story and my heart sinks a little. My teenage memories clash with my parental authority. I know how much fun I had when I was fifteen, but I want more for these girls. They have opportunities I didn't and like any parent, I hate the idea of them getting derailed before their lives have really begun.

"It's not that big a deal, Mom, Courtney is the only one who really got drunk."

"Where did you get the beer?" I ask.

"Some guy on Haight Street," Rose answers.

Cara rolls down the window and lets the cold air blow on her face.

"Why on earth did you get *that* kind of beer?" I ask.

"That's just what the guy bought us," Rhian says.

I understand someone being willing to buy beer for kids, but I am furious that anyone would buy two 40-ouncers of malt liquor for four tiny girls. I want to go find him. I want to lecture him. I want to take him to the hospital with us and show him what has happened.

"I can't believe you're complaining about the type of beer we were drinking," Cara says as we follow the ambulance into the hospital entrance.

We file into the hospital and Courtney is wheeled past us. Her face is wet with tears, she is strapped down to the gurney, a blood-soaked bandage around her foot. The other three burst into tears when they see her. They follow the gurney down the hall until the nurse shoos them away.

"Don't tell my dad, you can't tell my dad," Courtney shouts over and over.

I am the parent in charge here, and I have no idea what to do. I know Courtney's father is very strict and my first instinct is to cover for her. I wonder if I can just tell him she cut her foot and leave it at that?

One at a time nurses escort us into Courtney's room. She is somewhere between tucked and tied into a hospital bed with an I.V. in her arm and her foot propped up high. It turns out she is even drunker than they thought, and they've had to pump her stomach before stitching up her foot. She is sobbing and shouting and whispering. She is afraid and embarrassed. Over and over she says her father will kick her out of the house if he finds out she's drunk. I hold her hand and try to calm her down.

The nurse who's swabbing Courtney's foot starts to laugh. "I remember the first time I got drunk, my dad found me passed out in the hallway. Man, did I get in trouble. I must've been grounded for six months."

"See, Courtney, it happens to everybody," I say.

"Did it happen to you?" Courtney asks between sobs.

"Yeah, I drank so much once when I was about your age that I fell into a creek. I was wearing a long wool coat, and I can still remember lying on my back in the creek looking up at the trees, not being able to move because the coat was so heavy. Luckily it was a shallow creek and I landed on my back, or I probably would have drowned."

"Did you get caught?" Courtney asked.

"No, but I ruined my only coat."

One by one Rhian, Cara and Rose go and visit Courtney. Each of them returns to the waiting room devastated. Now on top of feeling angry and upset, I feel sorry for them. I'm scared and confused myself. I find myself desperately wishing for a rule book; something I can open to the section on Teenagers and Alcohol and find some instruction, wisdom, a proper admonishment, perhaps a chart with offenses in one column and recommended punishments in the other.

I look over at Denzil, who is thumbing through a torn *People* magazine, and I'm afraid that getting married to me must suddenly feel like a much more daunting proposition. I struggle to push away the fear that Denzil is going to run like a jackrabbit after encountering this part of my life head-on.

I feel awkward and a little guilty because when I spoke with Courtney's dad I told him she was just getting a few stitches in her foot and convinced him he didn't have to come down to the hospital. Five minutes later the admissions clerk, who also heard Courtney's wailing request not to tell her dad, and like me wanted to protect her, called me up to his desk.

"They just gave me a police report. I have to send a copy to the parents. They're going to find out she's drunk."

In other words, I'm busted. He hands me his phone and dials the number. When Courtney's dad answers I tell him we just found out that Courtney was a little drunk, and that he did need to come to the hospital after all.

I look at the girls sitting across from me slouched uncomfortably in the blue plastic chairs. I am amazed by how beautiful they are, even in this unfortunate state. I remember the lecherous stares and catcalls that haunted me when I was their age. I think about the high school teacher who took me into the woods and photographed me in skimpy clothes, and the history teacher who used to kiss me in the supply closet, and how misguided I was to feel flattered instead of violated. I think about the guy in the raincoat who tried to get me into his car, and the pickup I jumped out of while it was still moving after the driver unzipped his pants. I remember the freedom that came when I cut off my waist-length hair and men no longer paid as much attention to me.

I want to protect these girls. I don't want them to know any of these things. I feel painfully helpless and I have no idea what to do, how to behave, how to get them to listen to what I know without writing me off as just another pissed-off adult who doesn't understand. But I don't know what to do, so I start behaving like a pissed-off adult.

"I have one question for you girls," I say. "What the hell were you thinking?"

Denzil grabs my hand and squeezes. "That's a rhetorical question, Pam, they're fifteen, they just wanted to have a little fun and I'm pretty sure they know it was a

PAMELA HOLM

bad idea," Denzil says. "Don't you, girls?"

The three of them nod.

"But I'm guessing this won't be the last time one of you has too much to drink," Denzil says, "so here are a few pointers. You should never drink on an empty stomach. And if you are going to drink, it's a good idea to stay away from malt liquor, it'll mess you up bad. The amount that Courtney drank was enough to get a large man drunk."

"And if you decide to drink hard liquor," he continues, "you don't need to drink much. Only about this much," he holds his finger and thumb apart about and inch and a half. "And never, ever mix your alcohol. A drink is like a date, you stay with the same one all night."

I'm impressed. Denzil is obviously a parent waiting to happen.

"The thing is, girls, if you drink too much your judgment is shot and you can end up in really bad situations. If you drink enough you could black out, you could run someone over and not even remember it the next day. And boys—you've got to watch out for the boys—most of them are more than happy to take advantage of a girl who's drunk."

I realize I was wrong; instead of turning tail to run Denzil is giving advice to these kids about mixing their cocktails. He looks proud and parental, and every bit as protective, in his own way, as I am. Watching Denzil talk to the girls like this makes me feel like I've won the lottery.

# THE RINGS

"How can there be so many damn versions of a circle?"
Denzil asks after visiting the third jewelry store where
we've tried on every sort of wedding ring possible. Gold
bands with engraved Celtic knots, grapevines, tree
branches and festive floral patterns. Brushed platinum
bands with tiny rivets. Pounded gold with ruby inlays.
White-gold bands with bronze edging ranging in price
from $300 to $4,000.

Denzil and I have become uber-consumers. Our
every waking moment is devoted to shopping of one sort
or the other. Part of me is reveling in the role of bride,
while another part of me is resentful of all the time I've
spent planning and shopping. I struggle with guilt over
all the money we're spending. I'm still nursing a bad case
of buyer's remorse after dropping $250 on a pair of shoes
that I'll wear once. I've gone from starving artist to wal-
let-hemorrhaging wedding planner in too short a time to
make the necessary mental adjustments. I buy a $2,500
dress, then give money to anyone who shows up at my

door with a clipboard. I commit to $3,500 of flowers, then in an attempt to save money, I buy the 79-cent roll of aluminum foil instead of the one that's 98 cents.

Exhausted and a little confused, Denzil and I stop at the Burger Joint on Valencia Street and order our lunch at the counter. I look around at the bright red booths and the transparent green plexiglass that hangs above the counter and remember when Cara and I used to come here. I think about our friend, Tim, the recovering Marxist who used to manage the place. We'd come here for our version of a big night out mostly because it was nice to see Tim and partly because I knew he'd never let us pay. Cara would order, I'd pull out the money, place it on the counter, and Tim would slide it back to me with a smile.

This thought triggers a flood of memories. The pharmacist who used to give me asthma medicine refills when my prescription ran out because he knew I couldn't breathe and suspected I couldn't afford to go to the doctor. And the boyfriend who sent me to his doctor and had the bills sent to his office. I think about Robert, the acupuncturist, who treated me for migraines over two years without charging me a dime. Shu, my Chinese accountant with five kids of his own, who after doing my taxes and seeing my yearly income refused to let me pay him. I remembered when my friend Jeff pulled out his checkbook in my kitchen one night, wrote me a $1,000 check and told me that paying it back was optional. I remember the person I never got to thank for anonymously paying $500 of Cara's outstanding tuition bill. I think of Calvin and Kathy from my writing group, who bought me a cord of wood one winter when the pipes froze. Cork, who would hire me for every crazy job that came his way. I remember Mr. Weber, Cara's fifth grade teacher, who fought to keep her at the school by convincing the administration to give us a generous tuition-assistance grant. Every one of these gestures was deeply appreciated and instead of letting the gifts make me feel inferior or needy, I decided to see them as votes of confidence that made me feel loved.

I've reflected on each of these events, but never all at once. Stacked up one atop the other the effect is overwhelming. Tears come to my eyes and I think it's wrong to have thought of myself as a single mother all these years.

I've never blamed anyone for the situation I found myself in. I often made choices that made my life more difficult but the choices were conscious. I wanted Cara to have a better education than I thought the San Francisco public schools were going to give her. I also wanted to be able to take her to school and pick her up in the afternoon. Between drop-off and pick-up times I worked hard, and if we lived almost anywhere else in the country my income would probably be considered average. But San Francisco had become the dot-com boomtown and landlords were booting out tenants and raising rents all over town.

I live in appreciation of my new life. Denzil has been a good-luck charm. Since we've been together I've had more work than I can handle. At the same time Cara is a little older and more independent so my work hours aren't as dictated by her schedule as they once were. I have a deep belief that the moment you take your good fortune for granted it will go away. I fear that if you forget where you came from, you may get yanked back for a refresher course.

Denzil returns to the table with our food.

"How about we just get something simple?" I say

looking at my jade ring. "Simple rings, something not too expensive. The ring is really just a symbol and I'm not going to think you love me any more if I wear a platinum ring than if I wear a silver one." Simple rings will be my reality check.

# THE HONEYMOON

Denzil and I have decided to go light on the honeymoon because we're both eager to get back to normal life. We've been perusing web sites and getaway guides for weeks, looking for the perfect honeymoon hideaway.

We've decided on a few days at a small hotel called Manka's, along a saltwater inlet a couple of hours north of San Francisco. The place is charming and tucked into the heavy redwoods and neither of us has been there, which renders it neutral territory.

When I walk into Denzil's office to find the stapler, he is slumped in his chair in front of his computer surrounded by a thousand fragmented notes. A small brochure is laid out on the desk in front of him and he's talking on the phone. "The last time I was there," I hear him say, "there were a couple of cabins with outside showers..."

I glance at the brochure. It's tattered and scribbled on in Denzil's handwriting. The name "Manka's" is at the top. My stomach sinks.

"Have you ever been there?" Denzil asked me just yesterday.

"No, have you?" I said.

"No," he said.

I pick up the stapler and storm out of the room. I wish I wasn't so damn observant. I wish my mind moved a little slower than it sometimes does. Even when it's not in my best interest, I can detect lies and fibs, the slightest hesitation, the drop of a word, a sideways glance. A trait I inherited from my mother. I go back to my desk. I staple a stack of papers with enough force to nearly plow the stapler through my wooden desktop. My hands beginning to shake, my face grows hot. Denzil comes in, excited, unaware, or deciding not to notice, or hoping desperately that I haven't noticed the brochure or heard his conversation. Perhaps hoping his ebullience will wash out the reality of the situation.

"Okay, so we have a room booked at Manka's for two nights," he says.

I keep stapling, ka-bang, ka-bang, ka-bang. "Are you sure you've never been to Manka's?" I ask without turning around.

"No," Denzil says. "But I hear it's really nice."

"That's what I heard, too," I sneer. I stop stapling and turn around to face him, "Are you *sure* you've never been there before? Like maybe for a little romantic weekend with someone else?"

Denzil turns sheepish, he folds. "Yes, all right I went there with a woman I used to date, we went for a weekend and the place was so great and I really wanted to share it with you."

I didn't need quite this much information. "Let me get this straight, you want to take me, for our honeymoon, to a love nest you went to with another woman?

What the hell is wrong with you?"

"It was such a nice place, and I want to go there with you."

"No, the question was, what the hell is wrong with you?" Denzil is stung into silence.

"Forget it," I say, smashing the top of the stapler. "If you want to go stroll through your past you could have picked a better time than our honeymoon." I continue to staple.

"Worse than the monumental scale of your bad idea, is the fact that you lied."

That night I lie in bed next to Denzil, but I might as well be buried in a hole. I'm taken back to the tuxedo conversation, I'm not sure if bad judgment or naïveté is the common denominator. His apologies fall on deaf ears. I am unreachable. That afternoon I took a poll of my girlfriends. All agree Denzil's choice was misguided at best, but each of them followed this declaration with an anecdote of equal or greater audacity. One friend's husband bought her a full-length leather coat, then told her that all of his wives had worn them. She was number four.

What I remember most about my previous honeymoon was driving through Red Bluff, notoriously the hottest place in California, and for the first time ever actually feeling like I was going to die. My hungover husband was at the helm as I lay like a beached whale in the back of our 1967 Volvo station wagon, dipping towels into the cooler to soak up the melted ice water, and draping them across my large pregnant body, trying to coax the vicious hot breeze to cool me off. I was terrified that the car was going to overheat and I would give birth prematurely on the side of the highway in 104-degree heat. When we arrived at the bed and breakfast in

Ashland, Oregon, the proprietor scowled at my swollen belly and choked out a stiff congratulations before leading us to the honeymoon suite.

I know that Denzil spent a month in France on his previous honeymoon. As much as I don't want to feel bad about this, I do.

"Are you awake?" I whisper.

"Yeah."

I lie on my back and whisper to the ceiling. "I know you were trying to do something nice for us. And I know that you lied to me because you wanted to share something with me and you didn't want me to feel jealous. I know your intentions were good and you were only trying to protect me. I understand all these things, and at some point pretty soon I'll probably stop being angry. But for now you need to find somewhere else for us to spend our honeymoon."

"Okay."

"Good night."

# PARTY FAVORS

"What sort of favors are you going to have?" Jessica asks after dance class one evening.

"Favors," I say. "We haven't really talked about it."

I've always seen wedding favors as something you take home to throw away so you don't hurt the bride's feelings by leaving them lying around on cocktail tables at the reception.

"What sort of favors did you have?"

"We burned CDs of the two of us singing the songs we wrote for the wedding."

"Really?" I ask in disbelief.

I think of the pounding techno beat that permeates my house every evening. A couple of months ago Denzil got hold of a composition program for his computer. Since then our house has sounded like an all-night rave. Electronic music underlaid with Brazilian conga rhythms and shrill keyboard riffs. I'm warming to the music Denzil makes, I may even be starting to like it–at any rate it's become a recognizable soundtrack to my home life.

"I don't think we'll be doing that," I say to Jessica.

For the next several days I worry about the party favors. I think about the options and ask everyone I run into what their favorite wedding favors have been. One person says plastic flyswatters printed with the names and wedding date of the bride and groom. I lobby for yo-yos printed with our names. Denzil's only input is that he likes bubbles and he thinks the yo-yo idea is dumb.

Then I remember a party supply store that's next to the discount bridal store, a ratty little place in the industrial part of town. I drop by the store late in the afternoon, not to shop necessarily, but to look for inspiration.

Just past the register sits a glass case displaying dozens and dozens of favors. One shelf is filled with baby shower favors: tiny cradles wrapped in tulle and tied with printed ribbon; miniature baby bottles filled with confetti, small plastic baby booties. The glass shelf is dotted with spots where items have been removed, leaving ghostly clean spots in the dust.

The shelf below is devoted to wedding favors. Vows printed on parchment and threaded through silver and gold plastic wedding rings. Tiny bubble bottles in various shapes and styles. Colorful bundles of Jordon almonds, stale pastel obelisks no one is ever sure if they should eat or tuck in their underwear drawer.

I am overwhelmed. All of the favors are adorable. All of the favors are the tackiest things I've ever seen. These opinions live in me simultaneously, side by side, good ideas and bad ideas tucked into the same bed, their legs and arms tangled together like lovers. I'm confused. My artistic sensibilities have escaped me. My aesthetic standards have become muddied. Even I don't believe I make my living as an artist. I want to flee the store. My search for inspiration turns to obsession, obsession to panic. I wander through the aisles of fake foliage trying to clear my head. I breathe in the deep scent of plastic and oscillate between feeling like wedding favors are a stupid waste of money and that a wedding can't possibly be complete without them. I think about Jessica and Josh's CD and feel discouraged. The wall behind me is a riot of silk flowers, pink dahlias, blue irises, yellow zinnias, mauve roses, all bursting forth from plastic canisters. The colors lift me, and slowly I feel myself being seduced by my surroundings. Yes, yes, we need wedding favors. Wedding favors are great. I love wedding favors.

I remember that Denzil likes bubbles. He keeps a bottle in his car for road trips and traffic jams. Bubbles will make him happy, and if they turn out to be a bad choice, I can blame him. I stare at the shelf of bubbles. There are several designs to choose from: miniature champagne bottles; tiny church-shaped bottles with a removable steeple wand and a stained glass window sticker above the doors; a cylindrical bottle with a plastic dove taking flight on the top of the lid; a bottle in the shape of a wedding cake. I examine each design. The sector of my brain devoted to decision-making appears to be wearing out. Everything rests on a flat plane and I am unable to distinguish what is important and what isn't, what is good, what is bad.

I turn the plastic wedding cake bottle over and over in my hands, I tug on the bride and groom on the top of the cake, release the tiny bubble wand and blow. A shower of bubbles catches the light, the surfaces swirl with rainbow oil slicks. If I were five I'd think these glossy spheres were the coolest thing in the world. I am 38 and I still think they're the coolest thing in the world. I am insane. I grab six boxes of twenty bottles each, and take them up to the cashier before I have a chance to change my mind.

"Are you going to decorate these?" the clerk asks.

"Should I?"

"You don't have to, but they look more festive if you do."

The clerk, a Latino man in his sixties, steps out from behind the chipped linoleum counter and walks me to the window display at the front of the store, reaches into it and pulls out a handful of colorful lacy bundles. He holds them against his chest with his curved arm like a litter of rainbow kittens. One by one he holds the bundles up for me to examine. The plastic bottles are wrapped in one, two, and three layers of colored tulle, and festooned with printed ribbons announcing the name of the bride and groom, or wrapped with tiny roses attached by strands of wire. Little bursts of color. He's right, they are much more festive.

The clerk leads me over to a pegboard display of colored tulle circles packaged in cellophane and hanging from hooks. My head is ready to explode. More decisions. It doesn't matter, I tell myself. Of course it matters. Color is significant, color has meaning. Denzil's favorite color is blue, but that doesn't count. Every man's favorite color is blue. Blue is for boys. Purple for royalty. Orange for creativity. I try to remember the chakra colors—white for the crown chakra, yellow for the solar plexus, green for the heart. Ohsun, the African Orisha who represents love, is yellow; Yemeja, the ocean, the great mother, is blue. The sun is yellow, the earth is green, money is green. Suddenly I'm not just choosing a color, I'm choosing a pantheon of gods, I'm trying to settle on a whole system of belief.

On the way home when I'm stopped at a light I see

a homeless man who is missing three front teeth holding up a cardboard sign.

SPARE CHANGE OR FOOD,
THREE KIDS AT HOME,
DOWN ON MY LUCK.
GOD BLESS.

A familiar sadness tugs at me. I look at the box on the seat next to me and realize I'd like to help but I just spent all my cash on $80 worth of bubbles and white and purple tulle.

Later that night, I'm sitting on the living room floor enshrouding small plastic bottles in fabric. Denzil leans against the doorway staring at me with a confused look on his face. "Why are you doing that?" he asks.

"Because you wanted bubbles."

"I was talking about a couple of 69-cent bottles from Toys Я Us. Not the Martha Stewart craft hour."

"Hours." I correct, looking up from my stack of tulle, spools of ribbon and six boxes of bubbles. "Craft hours." I hold up a bottle to exhibit the incredible cuteness of what I am doing. "What do ya think?" I ask.

"I think you have gone insane. I think that you would be the first person to laugh and say how ridiculous those are if you weren't trapped in this weird bridal vortex."

"Well, I think they're cute," I say as I wrap one layer of white and one layer of purple tulle around another bottle and fasten it with a perfectly tied ivory ribbon.

# THE VOWS

The doorbell rings. It's Sunday morning two weeks before the wedding and we're meeting with Jonny Poynton, the minister who will perform the ceremony. Jonny is one of my best friends. We met nearly ten years ago at our children's school where Jonny and his wife Finola seemed as out of place as I did amid the gray-suited private school set. Jonny is an ordained minister for the Association for the Integration of the Whole Person. We have no idea what this means, but we've been assured he can legally perform wedding ceremonies.

"Can you get the door?" I ask.

Denzil flashes me a look that seems to say, "Why can't you get the damn door?"

"I have waffle batter all over my hands."

Denzil clomps downstairs like an angry eight-year-old. We've been at each other all morning. We argue about everything, we argue about nothing. Our heads are crowded with decisions to make, questions to be answered. And right now all of them seem important, life-changing, as if our future is riding on which color tablecloths we choose for the wedding dinner, which earrings I will wear and whether Denzil wears the blue or the gray tie. Nothing slips past without a snag. This attitude extends itself to everything around us, the slightest motion creates a debate: how much laundry detergent to use, how to fold the handkerchiefs, how long to beat the waffle batter. One step after the next is wrong. We are nervous and jumpy, testing each other, failing each other's tests.

Jonny comes into the kitchen with his usual bright cheer. He is tall and lanky and speaks with a British accent that's beginning to show signs of wearing off.

"So it's the countdown now," Jonny says. "Only three weeks to go."

"Two weeks, Jonny," Denzil corrects, with a hint of anxiety in his voice.

"Right, two weeks. Not much time left to back out. You two sure you want to go through with this?"

I look at Denzil and scowl. He bares his teeth like an angry baboon. This is probably a bad day for planning the ceremony. Right now, till death do us part seems like a very long time.

"Of course we want to go through with it," I bark a little too quickly, a little too loudly. Today we go on faith that love will resurface, just as it's been doing for the past year and a half. Love, adoration, anger and frustration all travel through us like phases of the moon. Large then small, disappearing entirely, then reappearing as a bright sliver that slowly grows back into a bright ball.

"You guys nervous yet?"

I lift my shirt and show Jonny the ripe bruise across my ribs. "I don't feel particularly nervous, but I did fall off a ladder two days ago and broke a $400 window in the process, and I nearly passed out while describing my dress to someone and I had a dream last night about the sun coming up on the wrong side of the sky."

"I'm only nervous that Pam is going to accidentally kill herself before the wedding," Denzil says.

The waffle iron beeps plaintively. I lift the lid and stab the golden disks with a fork and plop the waffles onto pink Fiestaware plates. I hand one to Jonny and the other to Denzil. I refill the waffle iron and lead them into the dining room.

"Okay, the way I see it," Jonny says between bites, "We have a few things to organize here. First, the general layout of the ceremony. Do you have any idea how you want to do this?"

Denzil and I stare blankly at each other.

"Jesus," I say, "I just realized we're going to have to get up in front of everyone we know and spill our most personal thoughts."

"It's called a wedding," Jonny says.

"I know, but it's so personal."

"Of course it's personal," Denzil says.

"But it's scary," I say.

"You've been through worse," Jonny says with little sympathy.

"I'll tell you what I don't want," I say. "I don't want one of those canned ceremonies that makes everyone so bored it looks like they'll fall out of their chairs before the bride and groom get around to kissing."

"And I don't want God, no mention of God," Denzil says adamantly.

"How about 'spirit'?" Jonny asks.

"Holy Spirit, no. Spiritual connection, maybe. And there'll be no sappy poetry, and no four-year-old ring bearer dressed in a midget's tuxedo."

"Yeah," I agree, "and none of that terrible ballpark organ music 'Here Comes the Bride' crap."

"Have you done any thinking about what you *do* want?" Jonny asks.

"Not really," Denzil admits.

"Me either."

"I think we should start out by me walking down the aisle burning some sage," Jonny says, "just to clear the space, you know, to help make it sacred."

Denzil and I both nod, happy for the least suggestion. Jonny does California hippie like only a foreigner can do. He is in his early forties, in transition between carpenter and spiritual therapist. He's wearing jeans and work boots and a colorful sweater, and has a batik scarf wrapped around his neck. His blue eyes are hemmed with deep crow's feet that make him look as if he's perpetually smirking.

"Is somebody going to walk you down the aisle?" Jonny asks.

"I haven't really thought about it," I say. I am lying; I've thought about it about as obsessively as I've thought about everything else: the shoes, the cake, the guest list and the music. I am aware of the tradition—the bride's father delivers his daughter to another keeper, the husband and the husband's family. He gives her over, gives her away. The very idea bothers me. It makes me feel like chattel. I moved out of my father's house when I was sixteen, he showed up five minutes into my first wedding, giving me away now seems a little late.

"No," I say to Jonny. "No one's going to give me away. I'll walk down the aisle alone."

"Okay. How about the vows?"

"Vows," I repeat.

"We talked about a no-minivan clause," Denzil says.

I shift nervously in my seat and then get up to check the waffles. It dawns on me that until now we've managed to avoid thinking about the actual content of the ceremony, and specifically the vows.

It suddenly seems obvious that all this activity, all the noise and chaos of planning a wedding, exists to camouflage the anxiety of actually getting married.

If we pour all our energy into deciding between raspberry or lemon filling, chocolate or buttercream frosting, is it possible to forget that sometimes we fight, really fight? Is it possible for me to overlook the fact that I will have to endure a lesson in wine-making every time we sit at a table of three or more people, for the rest of my life? In all the confusion, will Denzil be able to handle my tedious habit of tossing my wet towels on the bed? Can I forget that even the most minor money issues make Denzil hyperventilate, and can he ignore the fact that in twenty-five years I have never once balanced my checkbook? Will the confusion of the moment blind Denzil to the fact that he is about to become stepfather to a fifteen-year-old firecracker?

It's so much easier to think about whether or not to use rhinestone zippers for the bridesmaids' dresses and whether to serve sea bass or sole than it is to contemplate the leap of faith we are about to take, and the depth of the fall, should we miss our mark.

I walk into the kitchen pondering the question, "What does getting married really mean to me?" This isn't the first time I've thought to ask myself this question, but now, with the wedding two weeks away, it feels more poignant. And the more poignant it feels, the harder it is to focus on anything meaningful. The reality of the situation is daunting, so daunting that sober thoughts escape me. Only the giddy, shallow and most obvious ramifications of this major commitment come to mind.

Getting married means I won't be walking home at 6 a.m in an evening gown with my shoes slung over my shoulder. It means that finding a new boyfriend won't be my solution to boredom or depression or toothaches. Marriage means that the chances that Nick Cave will ever make me breakfast are seriously reduced. It also means I can stop thinking about being plucked out of my life by someone who drives a Ferrari and calls me *Paaameeela* in a toe-curling Italian accent. I'll live the rest of my life without knowing what it's like to have some heartbroken lover chase me through the airport, stop me as I'm about to board the plane and publicly declare his love. A declaration that would be peppered with phrases like "You'll never find someone who loves you like I do," and "If you get on that plane, you'll be making the biggest mistake of your life."

Suddenly I'm tempted to feel cheated, as if by getting married I'll miss a million golden opportunities. By choosing marriage I give up the fantasy of meeting that perfect stranger who will catapult me into a perfect life. The person, that one special person, the soulmate who destiny has led me to, the missing piece of my jigsaw puzzle, the man, that perfect man who will make everything okay. Blue skies forever.

I pour more batter into the waffle iron and laugh out loud when I think about how easy it will actually be to let go of my hollow fantasy. I can count the number of times I've stayed out all night on three fingers. I'm pretty sure Nick Cave is married. I have trouble taking people who drive Ferraris seriously. And I'd be embarrassed, and probably scared, if someone were to chase me down at the airport. I laugh because I've made that once-in-a-lifetime connection with that one "perfect" man more times than I can count. And I laugh because meeting Denzil was nothing like that. No thunderbolts, no angelic voices from on high, no anvil-dropping revelations. Just the quietly romantic truth that there is nothing I want that having Denzil in my life doesn't make better. *This* is why I'm marrying him in two weeks.

I walk back into the dining room with a fresh waffle. "I know why I want to get married."

"Because I don't complain about your waffles?" Denzil cracks.

"No, because there is nothing I want that having you in my life doesn't make better."

"Quick, write that down," Jonny says.

Denzil smothers his waffle in syrup and blows me a kiss.

We decide to work on the vows alone, then create the final draft together. For the next week Denzil and I ask each other daily how the vows are coming along.

"I'm working up to it," I answer.

"I'm making some notes," Denzil says.

We are both lying. This is hard. Public sentimentality makes me nervous. I aim to avoid it as much as possible for the simple reason that it makes me cry. Anything happy or slightly moving makes me cry. Brand-new puppies, babies in pink bonnets, listening to my daughter sing, all make me cry. I cry when my friends succeed, I cry when they get their hearts broken. I cry at weddings the moment the bride sets foot into the aisle. I'm a mess at funerals. I cry at movies and school plays. I tear up when someone strikes a minor chord on the piano. I don't like the fact that I am so easy to manipulate. Without my well-honed cynicism I'd spend all day with my face buried in a hankie. I imagine delivering my vows between sobs, and decide that's just going to have to be okay.

There are now ten days before the wedding and at this point I've put more effort into the wedding favors than into the ceremony. I've spent more energy on choosing the bubbles that our friends will toss into the nearest trashcan than on thinking about the vows that with any luck, I'll spend the rest of my life living up to.

I make, then break, appointments with myself to sit down and focus. Experience has told me that no matter how many heartfelt promises are made or what they are sealed with, whether it be diamonds, promises or children, if a marriage is making one or both parties miserable it will, and probably should, end. Then I wonder, if this is truly my belief, why am I getting married? Then I come around to thinking that a marriage commitment is about perseverance and good faith rather than the end result of happily ever after. No matter how many arguments we have, when the dust has settled and gentle words start flowing again, Denzil and I always come back to that same place of love. I'm committing to not walking away the moment things get rough. I'm committing to staying awake and not letting the relationship fade or get pushed out of the way by too much work and the challenges that arise when two people are trying to navigate their individual lives, as well as navigating a life together. Denzil and I are in total agreement about all these things, and that seems like a good start.

I procrastinate writing the vows by searching for a poem for Denzil's mom to read during the ceremony. I plop down on the bed and scour my dog-eared copy of Dorothy Parker poems, searching for something about love, marriage, happiness. I should know better, this is Dorothy Parker. For years, through bouts of depression, breakups and bounced checks, she was my companion, my internal voice surfing one heartbreak after the other. I never read Dorothy Parker to make myself feel better, but to make feeling bad more romantic and a little more bearable.

Denzil sits down on the bed beside me. "I've done it," he says. "I've written the vows."

"Just like that," I say, a little awed, "after days of procrastination, you've written the vows."

"Yup, you wanna hear them?"

"Okay."

Denzil stands up and begins to read:

"*Pamela, do you take Denzil to be your wedded husband, to love and to honor? And do you promise to yell louder as you both get older, to repeat everything three times because he won't go to the doctor to get his hearing checked, and to listen to his long-winded explanations of fake scientific phenomena? And through all this, never to complain (except for a little muttering under your breath now and then) about the day you promised to stay together for as long as you both shall live?*

"*Denzil, do you take Pamela to be your wedded wife, to love and to honor, and to nag about absolutely meaningless things like her seeming inability to hang up a coat when entering the house or hang up a wet towel after a shower? And do you promise to continue to clean up spills and broken glass that seem to follow her around like a lost puppy? And through all this, never to complain (except for a little muttering under your breath every now and then) about the day you promised to stay together as long as you both shall live?*"

I can't stop laughing. Loud peals of laughter bellow through the house. Tears flood my eyes, my asthma kicks up.

Denzil continues: *"Pamela, with this ring as a symbol of my vow, I hitch my star to your wagon and really, really hope you don't turn out to be some kind of reckless hussy just out for a good time.*

*"Denzil, with this ring as a symbol of my vow, I hitch my star to your wagon and really, really hope you don't turn out to be some sort of crazy drunken bastard."*

I'm still in hysterics. When I finally catch my breath it occurs to me that these vows really aren't that far off base.

"If you think about it," I say, "even though you were joking, those vows are really pretty accurate. Isn't that what marriage is about, dealing with all the annoying little things about each other while you live out the big picture? I mean, as romantic as getting married is, it isn't all butterflies and roses. Marriage is real and raw and these seemingly silly vows are more truthful than not. I say we use them, with a couple of minor changes."

"Really?" Denzil asks.

# BAD DREAMS AND LUCKY PARROTS

One week before the wedding I go to pick up my dress. I try it on just to check the final hemming. The hem is four inches too short. The seamstress tugs at it and calmly explains that dresses cut on the bias sometimes pull up when they are hemmed, like trimming your hair when it's wet. This doesn't explain why the bust and arms are tight. It's possible the stress of the wedding is making me gain weight, but I doubt it's making me taller. The seamstress suddenly looks up from my feet and says, "Oh my God, this isn't your dress." She shouts across the room to the girl at the desk. "Quick, call the woman who picked up her dress yesterday!" She looks back at me, "Oh Jesus, I hope she hasn't had it hemmed yet."

I leave the salon with the assurance that my dress will be returned and available for me to pick up in two days. I feel a little nauseated anyway.

I am a very efficient worrier; I can worry about a multitude of things without diminishing the intensity of any one. When I have a reprieve from worrying about my dress and the ceremony, I worry about the piping on the bridesmaids' dresses and our still-expanding guest list.

I've just found out sea bass is hovering near the endangered species list and I can't help feeling personally responsible, as eighty percent of our guests have requested sea bass over chicken or salmon.

I worry that I've hurt my mom's feelings. She offered to pay for the wedding photographer provided we hire an old friend of hers who's been photographing weddings since before I was born. He is eighty-two and currently recovering from his third heart attack. I'm pretty sure this would be a bad idea, so I sacrificed my mother's feelings and said no thanks. But now I feel like a jerk. I feel confident that I'm a good mother, and hopefully I'll be a good wife, but I'm a lousy daughter. It's been years since I've made the five-hour drive to visit my mother. Our relationship isn't volatile as much as unnerving. Yet as I grow older I see signs of compassion creeping in. Being raised by a fanatical Jehovah's Witness didn't make her life an easy one. Neither did growing up in Depression-era Canada without a father. And marrying my father, charming rogue that he is, only compounded her problems.

Wakeful worry gives way to bad dreams. I dream I am stuck in an elevator in my wedding dress which is held together with straight pins. I dream I'm wearing dreadlocks and a tiara for the wedding. I dream that our florist decorated the reception hall with dried gourds which are spray-painted gold and hung from branches with string. I dream my friend Morris comes out of our bedroom dressed in blue pajamas and tells Denzil that if he needs someone to sleep with me after the ceremony, he'd be happy to do it.

I wake at 3 o'clock in the morning worrying about the D.J. We've hired an old friend of mine to D.J. the wedding, an old boyfriend actually. We hired him because he has a great music collection and we are all mature adults and the past is the past. This seemed like an okay idea until right now at 3 a.m., when I'm convinced that this is the worst idea ever. In the wee hours, the situation snaps into focus and I realize I have left myself wide open for creative retaliation. I worry that Randall's going to play "I Think I Love You" by the Partridge Family instead of the Eric Satie piece with mandolin and cello which I've chosen for the processional. And the Everly Brothers' "I've Been Cheated" instead of the Carlinos Brown song I've chosen for the recessional; Gloria Gaynor's "I Will Survive" for the first dance instead of Jimmy Cliff's "I Can See Clearly Now."

As the big day draws near, I start to wonder what will go wrong. Will the florist really decorate the room with gourds and glitter-painted paper cups, will Denzil or I come down with the flu, will I trip over my train and fall ass over teakettle down the aisle? My mind works long hours manufacturing disastrous scenarios.

I can't help but think about my own experiences with other people's weddings. There was Tracy's wedding. Tracy had been my closest friend for more than ten years. A week before the wedding she called and asked me not to bring my boyfriend with me. Because he had already been invited, and because we had already booked a hotel room, and mostly because I was so insulted, I brought him with me to the wedding and never spoke to her again.

Tracy's wedding was followed by Lisa's. My 24-year-old friend was marrying her 63-year-old college professor, a wizened bitter man with a glass eye. A different boyfriend, who was very fond of Lisa, wrote her a little note reminding her to be sure not to let go of her own dreams. The glass-eyed professor intercepted the note, took it as personally as it was intended, and called our house shouting that if my boyfriend showed up at the wedding he would be physically removed. I went without him and stood in the back.

At Juliette and Marcel's wedding, a white dove was released during the ceremony and instead of soaring away majestically, it immediately plummeted into the San Francisco Bay. It was fished out of the water with a net, and despite a bridesmaid's valiant attempt at mouth-to-mouth resuscitation, it died.

Denzil and I had been together about six months when we went to Leo and Yvonne's wedding, where Denzil caught the garter and I caught the bouquet. Denzil theatrically pulled a handkerchief from his pocket, shook it out, then tucked it into the neck of his shirt before attempting the sliding-the-garter-up-the-leg ritual, which he decided to do using only his teeth. This wouldn't have been half as distasteful if he hadn't just officiated the wedding.

Tuesday before the wedding I pick up my dress, the right one. It fits perfectly. When I step out of the store I think, "This would be the perfect time for something auspicious to happen." I look up, half expecting the clouds to break apart and flood sunshine down onto the street. I look down the busy North Beach side street and want everyone to break into song and dance. Children spinning around lampposts, mailmen tap-dancing through crosswalks, hairdressers and their patrons singing sappy arias. I nearly skip down the street. I want to stop strangers and show them my dress. I want to tell them I'm getting married in four days.

I walk toward my car, and the cry of birds fills the air. It's faint at first, but grows louder and louder. It's the unmistakable screech of parrots. I stop in my tracks and crane my neck skyward. I can't believe it. This is exactly the kind of thing I was hoping for. A little piece of magic. Everyone on the street stops. People come out of cafés and bars and look up.

The parrots are deeply steeped in San Francisco urban legend. There are many stories of their genesis but my favorite is the story about a pet store owner setting them free when his pet shop caught fire. Over the years the flock has bred and been joined by other escapees, growing larger and noisier each year. The screeching becomes louder like a school bus of chattering children. Hundreds of green wings beat past overhead. The birds fly low, skimming the tops of the buildings. I decide to take the parrot sighting as a good omen, and of course I burst into tears.

# LET THE WILD RUMPUS BEGIN

The day before the wedding Luchi has a mountain bike race that runs late and puts her behind schedule for baking the cake. She bakes all the layers without incident. After they've cooled she sets out to frost them. The melted white chocolate that so easily rolled into a flat sheet and draped gracefully over the sample cake three days ago has now turned into a sticky mess. She spends the next two hours adjusting the recipe. Nothing works. She tries chilling the chocolate in the freezer before rolling it out. But when I come into the kitchen she's picking pieces of wax paper off the sticky ball of chocolate. I'm somehow confident she'll figure it out.

All morning people have been treating me like a powder keg of live explosives. I seem to be endowed with special wedding-day powers. I don't feel explosive, in fact I feel quite calm. They speak to me in soothing tones: "Pam, would like me to drive?" and "Would you like more sugar in your tea?" All the jittery excitement that has dogged me for months seems to have disappeared and I'm left with a deep glow, happy, thrilled, excited to be getting married. But I don't let on that I am fine, I don't want the special treatment to stop.

Christine, Cara and I arrive at the City Club at 10 o'clock for the 2 o'clock wedding. Kristy greets us in the lobby. She looks down at my bag overflowing with little bursts of purple and white tulle.

"Those aren't bubbles, are they, Pamela?"

"Yeah, aren't they cute?" I ask.

"Well, yes, they are quite cute, but I regret to inform you that our facility has a no-bubbles policy."

"How can anyone have a no-bubbles policy?" Christine asks.

I really hope this doesn't signal the decline into a series of wedding-day mishaps.

"The bubbles fall to the floor and the soap ruins the carpet."

"You're serious?" I say.

"Very serious, Pamela. If we were to let every bride who used our facility hand out bubbles to her guests we'd have gallons of soap dumped onto our floor every year."

I guess I can see her point. "Okay," I say.

"That's it, okay?" Christine says, "You're not going to fight even a little?"

"Nah, I figure I'm saving myself some embarrassment. I thought they were kind of goofy anyway."

We follow Kristy to the bride's dressing room. "I'm going to look at the bubbles as a sacrifice to the gods so that the rest of the day goes off without a hitch," I say to Christine and Cara.

"Mom, you're a dork."

"I'm your mother, I'm supposed to be a dork."

The City Club has supplied us with a dressing room,

a fruit plate, mineral water, a large-screen T.V. and a handful of movies. *The Wedding Singer, Royal Wedding, Breakfast at Tiffany's.*

Kerry, the hairdresser and makeup artist, gets started on Cara and Christine's hair, wrapping their heads into helmets of tight pin curls. They look like Kewpie dolls and I hope this is only a step in the beautification process.

I sit in a straight-backed chair having foundation applied to my face, one coat after another. I feel like a house being painted.

"This is so you can cry and not ruin your makeup," Kerry explains.

"That'll be helpful."

Cara pops *The Wedding Singer* into the VCR. I alternate between watching the film and staring out at the office building across the street. Within the first ten minutes of the movie Adam Sandler gets left at the altar. Until this moment being left at the altar hadn't crossed my mind and I can't believe there is something I forgot to worry about. My heart starts to race and I squirm in my chair while Kerry darkens my eyebrows. The calm I've been riding all morning shatters.

I realize, maybe for the first time amid the chaos of planning and preparing, exactly what is at stake. I am laying all my chips on one number. Everything from here on out, how I live, where I live, will be predicated on the promise I am about to make. This isn't a party anymore. It's not a celebration or a fun reason to get all our friends and family together. It's a huge leap of faith. I look down to the street ten floors below and feel dizzy.

Fear starts to set in, great washes of monumental, mind-spinning fear. My mind relives the failure of every failed relationship I've ever had. I think about Denzil's past catastrophes. I think about my dad's standard remark when I met someone new: *"You just gotta remember, Pam, everybody's single for a reason."* Why was Denzil single when I met him? Is there some great monster lying dormant, just waiting to blossom after he says, "I do"?

I turn my attention back to the movie. Adam Sandler's a wreck, he refuses to leave his bedroom.

"Cara, can you do me a favor and turn off that movie?"

"I'm watching it," she says.

"We'll, I'm living it, in my imagination anyway, and it's freaking me out."

Christine takes the movie out. "Okay, how about *Royal Wedding*–Fred Astaire, Jane Powell?"

"Does anyone get dumped?" I ask.

"Not that I remember." She slips the movie in.

"That would suck," I say. "To be left at the altar like that. I would hate to have that for a story. Things didn't work out, that's one thing; but he didn't show up for the wedding, that's another thing entirely."

"It rarely happens," Kerry attempts to assure me. "I've done hundreds of weddings, and I've never seen it happen, not once."

I shift uncomfortably in the chair. "Yeah, but planes do crash and someone does win the lottery. The odds are against it, but it does happen."

Christine sits on the floor in front of me, leaning her back against the window. "Pam, this is the part where you freak out. This is the part where you doubt everyone and everything, but you'll get over it. After Kerry is done with your hair and your makeup you're going to go take a walk around and see all the flowers, and see the D.J. and the band setting up, then you're going to put on your amazingly beautiful dress and nothing else is going to matter."

She's talking to me like I have a terminal illness, but I don't really mind—it's working. When my hair and makeup are done I wander around the City Club watching its transformation. There are flowers and candles everywhere. The dining room is set and beautiful. Every table is bursting with huge bouquets of flowers: dahlias, roses, yellow freesia. The band's instruments are tucked against one wall. Randall, the D.J., is loading milk crates of records off the elevator. He sets down a crate and gives me a big hug.

"This place is awesome and you look beautiful. I'm really happy for you and Denzil. See, everything works out like it's supposed to. It's all good."

I help Randall carry his records to the corner of the room, just to the left of the area we're using as the altar. The florist is busy constructing an arrangement that arches over the fireplace which will be to our backs during the ceremony. She's lacing yellow, orange and red flowers around smooth, bare branches, then weaving in spindly pomegranate branches, loaded with ripe pomegranates. Everything is stunning and I feel proud of the elegant playground Denzil and I have created for our friends and family.

When I come back into the dressing room Cara and Christine are dressed. Both are wearing full-length taffeta skirts, Cara's is olive green and Christine's is dark purple. Cara has a tight-fitting purple top with olive trim. Christine's top is the opposite, green with purple trim. Their hair has been taken out of the pin curls and falls in soft waves. They both look enchanting.

It's fifteen minutes before the wedding and a party has sprung up in our dressing room. Cara and her friends Rose and Rhian fuss with their makeup in the mirror. The flower girls, Denzil's niece Asunta, my niece Hailey and Malia's daughter Timothy, are fidgeting with their flower crowns. Hailey starts sneezing, and a ring of welts breaks out on her forehead. She begins to cry. My mother tries to convince her that she's fine, she's just allergic to the flowers, which makes her cry even more. Christine sits calmly talking to Kerry, who, it turns out, used to date Denzil's best man.

I grab Jonny and my silver flask of whiskey and we duck into the tiny smoking room next to the dressing room. The room is cozy and paneled with dark wood. A mural of an African jungle scene is painted across one wall. Tigers and monkeys frolic in the lush jungle setting. The mural looks like it was painted sometime in the 1930s, and right now it's the perfect distraction.

"How are you doing?" Jonny asks.

"I think I'm okay, I mean I still think getting married is a good idea, but I'm nervous as hell about the ceremony."

"It'll be over in no time. Just try to enjoy it."

He pulls out a chair for himself and one for me. "Here, sit down for a minute and just focus and think about your breathing."

I sit down and open the flask of whiskey, take a long sip, then hand it to Jonny.

"We've been through some stuff, haven't we?" he says.

"Sure have."

I think about how my life and Jonny's have woven together. Evan, a.k.a. the Angry Irishman, was Jonny's business partner. It was Jonny who arrived first and hid my passport after the British Guy, a.k.a., That British Bastard, hopped a plane to London. I've been the sob sister at the Poyntons' holiday dinner table more times than I care to remember, and I'm glad Jonny is going to be involved in an event in my life that doesn't call on him to act as cleanup crew.

"And now you're getting married. I'm so happy for you, Pammy."

I hear Christine's voice shooing everybody out of the dressing room. She knocks on the door to the smoking room, then pops her head in.

"Five more minutes of single life."

"Who's going to entertain me with stories now that you're settling down?" Jonny says, taking another slug from the flask.

"Who said anything about settling down?" Christine says, then takes a sip of whiskey.

Cara comes into the tiny smoking room. Seeing her sideswipes me with choked-up pride. She is radiant. Not just in the "of course my child is beautiful" sort of way, but a true beauty. Olive skin, large dark eyes, with long lashes and eyebrows that arch like two perfect punctuation marks. Cara has always been a pretty child, but now at fifteen, the soft roundness of her face is giving way to slight angles at the cheekbone and jaw and she becomes more stunning by the day.

In just a few minutes I am about to be expelled from the club of women who have pulled themselves up by their bootstraps, braving people's judgment and disapproving stares and pity. I've held my membership in this loosely knit club for more than twelve years. I understand the territory, I know the terrain, its secret passages and midnight hiding places. No matter how difficult the trials of single motherhood have been, they have been mine, familiar and understandable.

As happy as I am to have somebody with whom to share my life, I have to admit I am also reluctant to give up my parental autonomy. Aside from Gary, who is pretty agreeable and lives in a different house, I've never had to negotiate with someone about how to raise Cara, or defend my position on bedtimes or sugar consumption or curfews. I haven't had to incorporate someone else's opinions or beliefs into my game plan. I've never had to justify my actions. But however daunting it is for me to incorporate another person into my life, I know it is an even more life-changing proposition for Denzil to become a husband and stepfather.

I look at Cara and think it can't have been easy to have me for a mother. I always tried to keep her life on an even keel while mine was rocking and heaving all over the place, but I know I didn't always succeed. I just hope I managed to prolong the illusion that I knew what the hell I was doing until she was mature enough to weigh my failures against my successes. I grab Cara and pull her to my chest in a tight bear hug. "I love you, sweetheart."

"I love you, too."

I stand at the entry to the large room and watch Jonny walk down the aisle with sage smoke billowing around him. Our flower girls make their way down the aisle handing out roses to the guests they can reach. Tears well up in my eyes and obscure my vision for a few seconds before rolling down my cheeks. It's too soon. I can't do this yet. I've got an aisle to make it down in a somewhat dignified manner and I forgot my handkerchief. I take a deep breath, aiming to breathe into the emotion, to ride it and feel it instead of leaking it out my eyes.

Denzil follows, then Jerry, then Christine and Cara. The room is full of people and flowers and everything looks glorious. When Cara and Christine have made it to the altar I start to walk down the aisle. The music, "Gnossienne, no. 1," is perfect, strange and elegant. "Slowly, slowly, walk slowly," I say to myself over and over. I feel victorious. Thrilled that my crazy path has somehow led me here. All of our guests turn toward me and I start to laugh, loud howls of laughter. The room is filled with people I love, some of whom I haven't seen in years. I want to stop and say hi. I clutch my bouquet like a life raft as I walk slowly, slowly, slowly.

I look directly at Denzil for the first time today. He looks handsome and radiant standing up there with an elegant lily pinned to his lapel of his new suit. A beautiful smile lights his face, and I am deliriously happy that he's my future. From this day forward every decision I make will take this other person into consideration. I'll never share my body with anyone other than him. I'll fall asleep and wake up with him almost every day for the rest of my life. I'll argue with him, and make up with him, and grow and change over the years with him. He will be the constant in Cara's and my life. And it's the strangest thing but none of this scares me. I think about the parrots outside the dress shop, and Denzil's smile the first time we met, and everything we've been through since. Tears are streaming down my face and I don't care. When I reach the end of the aisle I hand my flowers to Cara and take Denzil's hands.

The ceremony was electric and overwhelming. The dinner was delicious. The toasts were kind and not too long-winded. In true Luchi fashion, she pulled off a last-minute save, and the cake was divine. Our friend Blake stood up and recited a poem she'd written titled, "Honey Moon." I thought it was beautiful, and yes, it made me cry again.

Randall the D.J. didn't extract his revenge. Cara danced with Adam, and weaseled drinks out of our friends. The Brazilian band played better than I'd ever heard them. The dance floor was crowded from the moment the music started. By the end of the night, shirts and dresses were soaked with sweat and a pile of shoes littered the edge of the dance floor. I danced with Denzil. I danced with my dad and with Jonny. I closed my eyes and let the music carry me into my new life.

### Honey Moon

Marry her moon
and she will wrap herself around you
like a gown of sun
love your shadow
as much as your pearled mirror
never forget you when the sky
tires of your glory
calls out the clouds

she longs for a lover
who isn't afraid of her howling
sees her waxing and waning
with equal eyes
a mate who lays with her some nights
leaves her alone on others
always offers a sliver to hold onto
the changing tide
her womb

Marry her moon
and she will never be lonely again.

— Blake More

# AFTER

I love being married. It's more and better than I hoped it would be. The stability of marriage has allowed all three of us to launch into our own creative endeavors. Denzil's drum kit takes up half the living room. Cara is reading Noam Chomsky and looking for colleges. I'm writing, playing percussion in a Brazilian band, and getting used to the idea that my daughter is growing up.

For months after the wedding we received thank you notes from charities all over the world. A home for retired nuns in London, the Pine Forest Preservation Fund, The Cancer Society, Project Open Hand. Someone even donated a pig to an African family in our name.

No one gave us a toaster.

## ACKNOWLEDGMENTS

I'd like to thank my husband, Denzil, for giving me the loving support that made it possible for me to write this book and my daughter, Cara, whose grace and strong will continue to amaze me.

A thank you to the folks at MacAdam/Cage for calling me at just the right moment. Especially my editor, Anika Streitfeld, whose thoughtful insight made this a better book.

A special thank you to all the people who so graciously let me use their real names and allowed me to write about the places where our lives intersected.